The Winter's Tale

ARDEN STUDENT SKILLS: LANGUAGE AND WRITING
Series Editor
Dympna Callaghan, Syracuse University

Published Titles
Antony and Cleopatra, Virginia Mason Vaughan
Hamlet, Dympna Callaghan
King Lear, Jean E. Howard
King Richard III, Rebecca Lemon
Macbeth, Emma Smith
Much Ado about Nothing, Indira Ghose
Othello, Laurie Maguire
Romeo and Juliet, Catherine Belsey
The Tempest, Brinda Charry
Twelfth Night, Frances E. Dolan
A Midsummer Night's Dream, R. S. White
As You Like It, Abigail Rokison-Woodall
King Lear, Jean E. Howard

The Winter's Tale

Language and Writing

Mario DiGangi

THE ARDEN SHAKESPEARE
LONDON • NEW YORK • OXFORD • NEW DELHI • SYDNEY

THE ARDEN SHAKESPEARE
Bloomsbury Publishing Plc
50 Bedford Square, London, WC1B 3DP, UK
1385 Broadway, New York, NY 10018, USA
29 Earlsfort Terrace, Dublin 2, Ireland

BLOOMSBURY, THE ARDEN SHAKESPEARE and the Arden Shakespeare logo are trademarks of Bloomsbury Publishing Plc

First published in Great Britain 2022
This paperback edition published 2024

Copyright © Mario DiGangi, 2022

Mario DiGangi has asserted his right under the Copyright, Designs and Patents Act, 1988, to be identified as the author of this work.

Cover image: Shakespeare, William, *Mr. William Shakespeares Comedies, Histories, & Tragedies*. (British Library's first folio, p. 287) © The British Library

All rights reserved. No part of this publication may be reproduced or transmitted in any form or by any means, electronic or mechanical, including photocopying, recording, or any information storage or retrieval system, without prior permission in writing from the publishers.

Bloomsbury Publishing Plc does not have any control over, or responsibility for, any third-party websites referred to or in this book. All internet addresses given in this book were correct at the time of going to press. The author and publisher regret any inconvenience caused if addresses have changed or sites have ceased to exist, but can accept no responsibility for any such changes.

A catalogue record for this book is available from the British Library.

A catalogue record for this book is available from the Library of Congress.

ISBN:	HB:	978-1-3501-7554-9
	PB:	978-1-3503-2252-3
	ePDF:	978-1-3501-7556-3
	eBook:	978-1-3501-7555-6

Arden Student Skills: Language and Writing

Typeset by Integra Software Services Pvt. Ltd.

To find out more about our authors and books visit www.bloomsbury.com and sign up for our newsletters.

CONTENTS

Series editor's preface vii
Preface ix

Introduction 1
    What is a winter's tale? 1
    The Winter's Tale and comedy 7
    The Winter's Tale and tragedy 14
    Sources, intertexts, allusions 20
    Writing matters 26

1   Engaging the language of the text(s) 37
    The texts of *The Winter's Tale* 37
    Listening to the language of the opening scene 40
    Editorial interventions: Spelling, capitalization, punctuation 43
    Editorial additions: Stage directions 50
    Fallen language in *The Winter's Tale* 52
    Writing matters 60

2   Language: Style and form 65
    Prose, verse and rhyme 66
    Analysing Shakespeare's blank verse 72
    Soliloquies 79
    Hermione's oration 86
    Reporting 87
    Writing matters 90

3   Language and history 97
    Women's speech and authority 97
    Obedience and resistance 103
    Festive pleasures, festive dangers 111
    Faith, magic and art: The statue scene 119
    Writing matters 130

4   Writing and language skills 141
    Choosing an essay topic I 141
    Choosing an essay topic II: Creative approaches 147
    Writing the essay 148

Bibliography 159

SERIES EDITOR'S PREFACE

This series puts the pedagogical expertise of distinguished literary critics at the disposal of students embarking upon Shakespeare Studies at university. While they demonstrate a variety of approaches to the plays, all the contributors to the series share a deep commitment to teaching and a wealth of knowledge about the culture and history of Shakespeare's England. The approach of each of the volumes is direct yet intellectually sophisticated and tackles the challenges Shakespeare presents. These volumes do not provide a shortcut to Shakespeare's works but instead offer a careful explication of them directed towards students' own processing and interpretation of the plays and poems.

Students' needs in relation to Shakespeare revolve overwhelmingly around language, and Shakespeare's language is what most distinguishes him from his rivals and collaborators – as well as what most embeds him in his own historical moment. The Language and Writing series understands language as the very heart of Shakespeare's literary achievement rather than as an obstacle to be circumvented. This series addresses the difficulties often encountered in reading Shakespeare alongside the necessity of writing papers for university examinations and course assessment. The primary objective here is to foster rigorous critical engagement with the texts by helping students develop their own critical writing skills. Language and Writing titles demonstrate how to develop students' own capacity to articulate and enlarge upon their experience of encountering the text, far beyond summarizing, paraphrasing or 'translating' Shakespeare's language into a more palatable, contemporary form. Each of the volumes in the series introduces the text as an act of specifically literary language and shows that the multifarious issues of life and history that Shakespeare's work addresses cannot be separated from their expression in language. In addition, each book takes students through a series of guidelines about how to develop viable undergraduate critical essays on the text in question, not by delivering interpretations but rather by taking readers step by step through the process of discovering and developing their own critical ideas.

All the books include chapters examining the text from the point of view of its composition, that is, from the perspective of Shakespeare's own process of composition as a reader, thinker and writer. The opening chapters consider when and how the play was written, addressing, for example, the extant literary and cultural acts of language, from which Shakespeare constructed his work – including his sources – as well as the generic, literary and theatrical conventions at his disposal. Subsequent sections demonstrate how to engage in detailed examination and analysis of the text and focus on the literary, technical and historical intricacies of Shakespeare's verse and prose. Each volume also includes some discussion of performance. Other chapters cover textual issues as well as the interpretation of the extant texts for any given play on stage and screen, treating, for example, the use of stage directions or parts of the play that are typically cut in performance. Authors also address issues of stage/film history as they relate to the cultural evolution of Shakespeare's words. In addition, these chapters deal with the critical reception of the work, particularly the newer theoretical and historicist approaches that have revolutionized our understanding of Shakespeare's language over the past forty years. Crucially, every chapter contains a section on 'Writing matters', which links the analysis of Shakespeare's language with students' own critical writing.

The series empowers students to read and write about Shakespeare with scholarly confidence, and hopes to inspire their enthusiasm for doing so. The authors in this series have been selected because they combine scholarly distinction with outstanding teaching skills. Each book exposes the reader to an eminent scholar's teaching in action and expresses a vocational commitment to making Shakespeare accessible to a new generation of student readers.

Professor Dympna Callaghan
Series Editor

PREFACE

The Winter's Tale is a play that many people are likely to encounter later in their educational careers. Unlike *A Midsummer Night's Dream*, *Romeo and Juliet*, *Hamlet* or *Macbeth*, *The Winter's Tale* is a rare presence in secondary school English curricula. It certainly doesn't have the cultural currency of these other plays – as measured by immediately recognizable quotations, characters or plots. Nor can it boast a big-budget, star-studded film version, such as Kenneth Branagh's *Hamlet* (1996), Trevor Nunn's *Twelfth Night* (1996), Michael Hoffman's *A Midsummer Night's Dream* (1999) or Julie Taymor's *The Tempest* (2010), not to mention popular adaptations such as *O* (2001), based on *Othello*, or *She's the Man* (2006), based on *Twelfth Night*. There are good reasons for the relative unfamiliarity of *The Winter's Tale*: its length, ambiguous genre, difficult language, sprawling sixteen-year plot, extensive pastoral episode and use of stylized romance motifs. These very qualities, however, also make *The Winter's Tale* a fascinating play that repays careful reading and study. Making this challenging play accessible to students, this book will help you to engage with Shakespeare's language as a way into his complex and timely explorations of gender, sexuality, politics, aesthetics and religion. Each main chapter concludes with a 'Writing Matters' section that gives you many opportunities to use writing to practice the interpretative skills and strategies introduced in the chapter.

As I mentioned above, *The Winter's Tale* is characterized by an ambiguous genre that combines comic and tragic elements, along with a healthy dose of the wonderful and supernatural. In the Introduction, we will explore the 'language of genre' in the play: Shakespeare's use in *The Winter's Tale* of the kinds of language that he had developed in his earlier comedies and tragedies. For instance, the presence in *The Winter's Tale* of witty repartee between men and women harkens back to comedies such as *Taming of the Shrew* and

As You Like It; arguments about political counsel and the limits of monarchical authority revisit issues explored in tragedies such as *King Lear* and *Macbeth*. Having considered Shakespeare's earlier plays as a kind of linguistic and thematic 'source' for *The Winter's Tale*, we will then address what Shakespeare borrowed and changed from the play's direct source, a sixteenth-century English prose tale called *Pandosto*.

Chapter One, 'Engaging the language of the text(s)', moves from the broad issues of genre, influence and source to a more focused analysis of the play's language. It begins with an examination of the kinds of changes that modern editors make to the originally published texts of Shakespeare's plays. Knowing about those changes can help you read the plays more insightfully. Insightful reading begins with paying close attention to the language used by various characters, beginning with the opening scene, which we will examine in some detail. Throughout the chapter, we will analyse small units of meaning such as individual words and even punctuation marks. We will also address the play's exploration of thwarted verbal communication, particularly visible in convoluted language about female sexuality.

In Chapter Two, 'Style and form', we shift from smaller units of meaning to the styles and forms of language – prose, verse, soliloquy, oration, reporting and rhetorical figures – that give Shakespeare's plays their verbal variety and texture. We begin with the two basic media of dramatic writing: prose and verse (both rhymed and unrhymed). When does Shakespeare use prose or verse, and with what effects? We will spend some time practising close analysis of Shakespeare's unrhymed dramatic verse, paying attention to poetic meter, lines and sounds. Then we will turn to some of the major forms of speech used by characters in *The Winter's Tale*: soliloquy, oration and reporting. We will delve into the various rhetorical strategies that characters use to express themselves and to persuade others of their beliefs.

Chapter Three, 'Language and history', introduces strategies for producing original readings of *The Winter's Tale* in historical context. By reading episodes from *The Winter's Tale* alongside contemporary texts such as sermons, conduct manuals and political treatises, we will explore how the play addresses volatile issues concerning gender, politics, religion and popular entertainment. Paulina's outspokenness will be the focus of our discussion of women's agency in the patriarchal world of the play (and Shakespeare's culture). Paulina's bold confrontation of her king will also inform our consideration of early modern political thinking on the limits and abuses of monarchical authority. What are the expectations for obedience and the possibilities for resistance when subjects are ruled by an unjust king? Turning to Act Four of the play, we will consider how Perdita's anxiety about dressing up and theatrical play resonate with early modern attacks on the social and moral disorders of the public theatre. How do contemporary objections to stage acting echo the suspicions of female sexual transgression in the play? The chapter concludes with a discussion of the complex intertwining of religion, magic and art in the play's last scene, centred on the animation of Hermione's statue. Understanding the overlapping languages of the theological, supernatural and aesthetic is essential for appreciating the tragicomic atmosphere of wonder and mystery that brings the play to a close.

Building on previous 'Writing Matters' units, the book's final chapter, 'Writing and language skills' offers more opportunities to practise your writing, research and interpretive skills. Much of the chapter focuses on the challenge of identifying strong essay topics. Strategies discussed will include mining a reading journal, focusing on a single word, discussing a modern adaptation of the play, analysing a performance of the play and engaging with critical perspectives. I also provide some more 'creative' options for essays. The final section of the chapter provides strategies for composing the various parts of an essay: the title, introductory paragraph, thesis statement, main paragraphs and concluding paragraph. Along the way, I offer tips for quoting and analysing passages from Shakespeare that should strengthen any essay.

Some final words for clarity. Throughout this book, I refer to 'early modern', the term that historians use to designate the period from 1500 to 1800 in Europe. When I refer to 'early modern England', I generally mean sixteenth- and seventeenth-century England, particularly the years in which Shakespeare was contributing to the vitality of the London theatre (*c.* 1590–1614). I use 'contemporary' for Shakespeare's period and 'modern' for our own. Sometimes in my citations from sixteenth- and seventeenth-century texts, you will note that instead of page numbers I provide 'sig' letters and numbers. 'Sig' stands for 'signature', which refers to a standard feature of early printed books: the gathering of sheets of paper into groupings marked by letters and numbers (e.g. A1-A4, B1-B4, C1-C4 etc.). Printers used signature marks to help them assemble pages in the correct order. A letter indicates where a particular gathering falls in the series of gatherings (so A is the first gathering, B the second etc.); a number indicates the particular leaf within a gathering (first, second, third etc.). Finally, in the designation 'A1r', 'r' stands for 'recto' or the 'right' (first) side of the leaf; in 'A1v', 'v' stands for 'verso' or the inverse (second) side of the leaf. For ease of reading, when quoting early modern texts I will modernize, i.e. change punctuation and spelling to conform to the conventions of modern English.

Since *The Winter's Tale* is a late play of Shakespeare's, there are times when I will refer to earlier comedies or tragedies to contextualize what is happening. Although I will provide quotations from those plays, you might also wish to have access to them through a complete edition such as the *Arden Shakespeare* or *Norton Shakespeare* or through individual volumes published by Arden, Oxford, Cambridge, Bedford or Folger. My citations from *The Winter's Tale* are from the Arden Shakespeare volume edited by John Pitcher. All citations from other Shakespeare plays are from the *Arden Shakespeare Third Series Complete Works*.

Introduction

The language of genre

What is a winter's tale?

The Winter's Tale insistently calls attention to its own status as a piece of fiction. Late in the play, when Perdita's true identity as the princess of Sicily has been revealed, members of Leontes's court share the news of this stunning discovery. One Rogero admits that '[t]his news which is called true is so like an old tale that the verity of it is in strong suspicion' (5.2.27-9). Although the court vouches for the 'verity' or truth of the news, these strange events so resemble 'an old tale' that they strain belief. The word 'tale' here might remind of us a fairy tale: imagine your scepticism if you read a social media post from an acquaintance who claimed to have married a prince after having lost her shoe at a ball. Later in the same scene, responding to Rogero's query about the strange death of Antigonus, the Steward replies, 'Like an old tale still, which will have matter to rehearse though credit be asleep and not an ear open' (5.2.60-1). Tellers of old tales never lack strange 'matter to rehearse' (events to report) even if nobody is listening or wouldn't 'credit' (believe) the story if they were. In short, the Steward suggests that old tales have a life of their own: an ability to reproduce or recycle their materials despite the fact that they strain belief. In a fairy tale or folktale, the very familiarity of events – magical transformations, a stepmother's treachery, gruesome deaths, reversals of fortune – cues us to the presence of fantasy. Fairy tales and folktales do seem to have lives of their own, in that their stock elements have persisted over centuries across different cultures.

As the play's title suggests, Shakespeare draws upon 'old tales' in *The Winter's Tale* (Belsey, 'Exiled' 162). According to the *Oxford English Dictionary*, an important resource for understanding what English words meant in the past, the phrases 'fairy tale' and 'fairy story' first show up in mid- to late-seventeenth-century English texts, decades after Shakespeare's death, to describe stories with 'fantastic or magical' elements [*OED*, fairy tale A. *n*., 1.]. In early modern England, 'faith in various forms of magic, including fairies, appeared to linger especially in rural areas despite a general decline of belief in magic'; so while 'fairy belief existed, it was far from universal' (Lamb 35). As Mary Ellen Lamb details, rural people used fairy belief as 'white lies to refer to shared understandings about "found" money and sexual acts' (36). For example, when in *The Winter's Tale* the old Shepherd discovers the infant Perdita accompanied by a box of gold, he believes her to be the illegitimate, abandoned child of a serving woman. Nonetheless, he protects Perdita 'from the shame of her origin' by telling his son that she is a 'changeling' child abducted or abandoned by the fairies (Lamb 33; 3.3.120). Moreover, the Shepherd justifies keeping possession of the found treasure by calling it 'fairy gold' (3.3.120). Although it is difficult to assess what people of the past believed, it is evident that fairy stories were sometimes fantastic tales told to children and at other times cover stories used to occlude actual crimes or instances of abuse – such as the abandonment of an infant to her presumed death.

Significantly for *The Winter's Tale*, in which a king emphatically rejects the truthfulness of women's speech, a common term in Shakespeare's time for a patently fictional story was 'old wives' tale'. In *The Old Wives' Tale* (1595), a play by Shakespeare's contemporary George Peele, an old blacksmith's wife tells two boys a 'merry winter's tale' about a princess who is captured by a sorcerer (Lamb 58). The title of *The Winter's Tale* evokes the stereotypical setting for such a domestic scene: an older woman – usually a wife, maid or nurse – surrounded by children at a winter's fire (Belsey, 'Sad' 4). In *Macbeth*, Lady Macbeth acidly compares her frightened husband to a child who pays too much heed to a 'woman's story at a winter's fire / Authorized by her grandam' (3.4.62-3). Only a child would believe a ghost story 'authorized' or invented by a foolish old grandmother and delivered by another woman to pass the time during a cold night. The seventeenth-century biographer John Aubrey confirms that in his childhood 'the fashion was for old women and maids to tell fabulous stories night times and of sprites, and walking of ghosts' (qtd. Fox 188). In sum, the term 'old wives' tale' conveys the belief that women's speech is, to quote Lady Macbeth, less 'authorized' and credible than male speech or writing. According to Lamb, the 'contempt for women's lore expressed in the phrase "old wives' tales" reflected a gender system inherent in the all-male grammar schools burgeoning in England between 1560 and 1660' (52). In the final scene of *The Winter's Tale*, Paulina admits that she would be dismissed as precisely such a foolish old woman were she to claim that the statue of Hermione had come alive: a story so incredible (in the etymological sense of 'difficult to credit') would be laughed at '[l]ike an old tale' (5.3.117).

Like the play's title, Paulina's reference to an old tale draws our attention to the fact that *The Winter's Tale* itself resembles a fairy tale. In the final scenes of the play, three references to 'old tales' describe three events that are incredible in different ways: the wonderful return of Perdita to her country of birth, the grotesque death of Antigonus at the claws of a bear and the miraculous resurrection of Hermione, believed dead for sixteen years. Collectively, these events mix joy with sorrow. Hermione's reunion with her family is tempered by the memory of her sixteen-year absence from them. Likewise, the joyful news of Perdita's return is mitigated by sorrow at the report of Antigonus's death. Suspended between 'joy and sorrow', Paulina has 'one eye declined for the loss of her husband, another elevated' for the return of Perdita (5.2.72-4). During the unfolding of tragic events early in the play, Mamillius informs his mother that 'a sad tale's best for winter' and begins to relate a 'sad' (sorrowful or serious) story of 'sprites and goblins' in a 'churchyard' (2.1.25-6, 30). Ghosts and graveyards fit the time of year commonly associated, particularly in an agricultural society such as Shakespeare's, with loss, suffering and death. In sum, the old tales told or alluded to in the play by little children, women and gossiping courtiers convey various moods: they are sad, frightening, ridiculous, wonderful, joyful and grotesque. These old tales are the polar opposite of the oracle authorized by the (male) god Apollo, ritualistically recorded, sealed and delivered by two lords, and taken as absolute truth by everyone but the unhinged monarch.

We are approaching an important insight about the mixed genre of *The Winter's Tale* that we will continue to explore below. The old tales told by Shakespeare and by his characters combine comic and tragic elements: they encompass joy and sorrow, loss and restitution, life and death, betrayal and forgiveness. When Shakespeare was writing *The Winter's Tale* (c. 1609–11), a new kind of drama called tragicomedy was becoming popular on the London stage. As Valerie Forman explains, the core tension of tragicomedy is 'the relationship between two potentially opposing genres – one that foregrounds loss, and the other resolution' (1). Structurally, tragicomedies are comedic in that they conclude in celebration and reunion, but they include tonally tragic episodes involving events such as war, death, incest, political turmoil and intense psychological suffering. The four plays that Shakespeare wrote or co-wrote between 1608 and 1612 – *The Winter's Tale*, *Pericles*, *Cymbeline* and *The Tempest* – share these characteristics to different degrees. Shakespeare's co-author John Fletcher defined tragicomedy not as a play containing 'mirth and killing', but as a play that lacks deaths, 'which is enough to make it no tragedy, yet brings some near it, which is enough to make it no comedy' (sig. A3v). As Gordon McMullan and Jonathan Hope argue, it's a mistake to take Fletcher's definition as true of all tragicomedy, since it was intended only to justify the theatrical failure of his pastoral tragicomedy *The Faithful Shepherdess* (4). Despite Fletcher's pronouncement that tragicomedies avoid death, plays such as *The Winter's Tale* and *Cymbeline*, in which major characters die, might be considered tragicomic in mood and structure. Writing mainly of plays written after 1610, Walter Cohen offers a more politically oriented description of tragicomedies as plays that are 'concerned with kings and their courts… [and] find the royal setting defective, and in every case the defects are remedied by the end of the action' (131-2). How might Cohen's view of tragicomedy work as an account of *The Winter's Tale*?

Another term commonly used today for *The Winter's Tale*, *Pericles*, *Cymbeline* and *The Tempest* is 'romance', a 'notoriously slippery category' (Fuchs 1). The Victorian editor Edward Dowden first devised this categorization for Shakespeare's late plays. As Cyrus Mulready shows, Dowden, influenced by English Romanticism, called these plays 'romances' because he believed that they manifested the workings of a mature 'spiritual' imagination free from the formal strictures of classicism (37-8; see also Mowat, 130-3). Following Dowden's innovative separation of these four plays from Shakespeare's earlier work, anthologies of Shakespeare's plays continue to categorize them as 'romances'. In early modern Europe, however, 'romance' usually referred not to drama but to a 'fictional *narrative* form'; moreover, for early moderns 'romance' was not, of course, temporally post-Romantic, as it was for Dowden, but post-classical and post-medieval (Mulready 46; Cooper 5-7). Not a distinct genre as much as a set of themes and conventions – a 'literary and textual *strategy*' (Fuchs 9) or a collection of 'memes' (Cooper 4) – early modern romance derived from three different literary traditions: Greek novels written in the third century CE (Gillespie); medieval chivalric poems about the heroic deeds of travelling knights (Cooper); and late medieval religious drama (Grantley).

What did these post-classical romances have in common? At the broadest level, romance typically involves a 'success story in which difficulties of any number of kinds are overcome, and a tall story in which they are overcome against impossible odds or by miraculous means' (Felperin, *Romance* 10). A good example of romance today is *Star Wars*: a small rebellion's unlikely victory is a 'success story' in which multiple difficulties (e.g. the overwhelming might, brutality and resources of the Empire) are overcome against 'impossible odds or by miraculous means' (e.g. by Luke Skywalker's use of the Force singlehandedly to destroy the Death Star). Focusing on the cross-cultural and cross-racial encounters of early modern romance, which often takes the form of a quest, Benedict Robinson writes that romance 'estranges the world it represents, suffusing its landscapes with wonder, with the marvelous or the miraculous' (4). Maurice Hunt provides an excellent account of the typical character types, events and values of Hellenistic romance. When reading Hunt's account, consider which of these elements inform *The Winter's Tale*. According to Hunt, romances usually consist of

> an episodic journey, of a hero's or pair of separated lovers' wandering toward home or reunion. Along the way, they endure a series of hardships, including shipwrecks and seizure by pirates, as well as marvels and the intervention in their lives of deities.... Usually the hero or heroine must disguise himself or herself, almost always as a person of a lower social class, at

one or more times during the quest. A token or mark generally precipitates the final union of romance between strangers, made so by lapsed time, great distances, and disfiguring suffering, who discover they are husband and wife or lovers.

(385)

As Hunt suggests, romances, like tragicomedies, are comic at their core: after a difficult quest or painful years of separation, the protagonists are rewarded with a joyful reunion or homecoming.

When Shakespeare's colleagues collected his dramatic work in a book that we now call the First Folio (1623), they included a 'Catalogue' that divided the plays into three distinct categories: Comedies, Histories and Tragedies. For unknown reasons, they did not include a category for tragicomedies, under which they might have placed *The Winter's Tale*, *Cymbeline*, *The Tempest* and even *Measure for Measure* or *The Merchant of Venice* (Lesser 135). *The Tempest* is the first and *The Winter's Tale* the last play listed in the Comedies section of the Catalogue. Jean Howard observes the 'instability' of these 'generic designations' (298). For instance, although *Richard III* is grouped with Histories in the Catalogue, the play text itself is titled *The Tragedy of Richard the Third*: history and tragedy thus seem to 'interpenetrate' each other instead of delineating distinct kinds of drama (Howard 298). Lawrence Danson argues that Shakespeare's consciousness of genre was 'active and unconfining', meaning that he deliberately attempted to 'diminish or conflate' generic distinctions (117, 102). Recognizing the inadequacy of 'comedy' to define *The Winter's Tale*, contemporary scholars have called it a 'romance', 'late play', 'late comedy', 'post-tragic play', 'comedy of transformation', 'comedy of forgiveness', 'tragicomedy', and even 'romantic tragicomedy' or 'tragicomic romance' (McMullan 2-4, 81; Mowat 133-4). As Stephen Orgel observes, '[c]omedies for us may be high or low and remain comedies, but those that are either not funny enough or too serious we remove from the category: hence *Measure for Measure* becomes a problem play, *The Winter's Tale* a romance' ('Kinds' 146). Some critics have even placed *The Winter's Tale* among those late plays that are 'beyond genre' or '*sui generis*' (McMullan 77).

Although generic categorizations are impure, they can nonetheless help us to recognize how a particular text deploys a set of conventions that it shares with other texts. In Howard's words, 'the utility of generic categories is less ontological than provisional and productive: that is, generic schema do not so much map essential and immutable kinds of writing as describe the historically produced and mutable conventions by which a certain *kind* of text is distinguished from other *kinds*' (298-9). In what follows, we will explore the 'historically produced and mutable conventions' of the different dramatic kinds to which Shakespeare contributed, with the aim of putting into action Howard's conclusion that genre 'is a concept that lets critics and readers make productive connections between texts' (299). In short, we are going to make productive connections between *The Winter's Tale* and some of Shakespeare's earlier comedies and tragedies.

The Winter's Tale and comedy

The Winter's Tale includes a comedic plotline familiar from Shakespeare's comedies: a father (here, Polixenes) prevents a young couple (his son Florizel and his love, Perdita) from getting married; the lovers evade punishment and eventually secure permission to marry. Variations on this plot are found in *The Taming of the Shrew*, *A Midsummer Night's Dream*, *The Merry Wives of Windsor* and *The Merchant of Venice*. Along with these common plot elements, Shakespeare's comedies also share similarities of language. Here, I will discuss three kinds of language typical of comedy: (1) the exchange of compliments, vows and doubts between young lovers; (2) the gendered combat of wits in which men and women mock or insult each other; (3) the declaration of forgiveness, joy or harmony among reunited family members or lovers.

Let's begin by considering what's in the name of a Shakespearean comedy. Shakespeare's tragedies usually identify only a central male protagonist (e.g. *Julius Caesar*, *Hamlet*, *Macbeth*, *King Lear*, *Coriolanus*); *Romeo and Juliet* and *Anthony and Cleopatra*, as love tragedies, are the exceptions. In the titles of comedies, it is more common to find plural characters and/or their place of residence: *The Merchant of Venice*, *The Two Gentlemen of Verona*, *The Merry Wives of Windsor*. The titles of comedies thus emphasize not the individual but the larger community: the worlds of Venice, Verona or Windsor. Even as it identifies a single character – the 'shrew' – *The Taming of the Shrew* implies the existence of another character who does the taming, and rather than identifying the titular 'shrew' as Katherina Minola it identifies a type of woman of which there are presumably many. Why would a communal emphasis be appropriate for a comedy? What might community have to do with the titles of some of Shakespeare's other comedies, such as *Love's Labor's Lost*, *As You Like It*, *Much Ado about Nothing*, *Twelfth Night*, *Measure for Measure* or *All's Well That Ends Well*? Note that several of these titles represent common sayings: they encapsulate a proverbial wisdom that implies a general consensus of belief. Other titles point to an event or occasion experienced by most of the characters in the play, or, in the case of *As You Like It*, seem to appeal to a theatrical audience's expectation of pleasure. In sum, the titles of Shakespeare's comedies suggest that these plays will address the conflicts or problems navigated by a group of people who share the space of a household, town, city or even a theatre. Even though *All's Well That Ends Well* contains a sovereign (the King of France), its title, unlike those of tragedies, doesn't identify him as the single privileged character of the play. Through its title, *The Winter's Tale* thus seems to share this communal or collaborative emphasis with Shakespeare's comedies: a tale requires one or more writers, speakers and listeners.

The language of comedy I: Courtship

Along with the communal implications of its title, *The Winter's Tale* features certain conventional kinds of language typical of comedy. Since we tend to think of Shakespeare's comedies as fundamentally about the process of courtship leading to marriage, we can begin with the language of wooing that is a staple of the genre. Sometimes in Shakespearean comedy, courtship occurs while one of the characters is in disguise. Let's take *As You Like It* as our example. In this comedy, the young heroine, Rosalind, must flee the court of her treacherous uncle. Accompanied by her cousin Celia, she escapes to the Forest of Arden disguised as a young man named Ganymede. There, Rosalind encounters a young man, Orlando, whom she had first met while at court. During that initial encounter, Rosalind and Orlando had both fallen for each other. Wishing to flirt with

Orlando while still disguised as Ganymede, Rosalind determines to speak to him 'like a saucy lackey' or impertinent servant, a performance that requires witty, satirical language (3.2.290). Rosalind uses this language both to test Orlando's sincerity in love and to engage in flirtatious banter. Speaking of Orlando himself, Rosalind/Ganymede informs Orlando that '[t]here is a man haunts the forest that abuses our young plants with carving "Rosalind" on their barks... [i]f I could meet that fancy-monger I would give him some good counsel, for he seems to have the quotidian [fever] of love upon him' (3.2.349-55). When Orlando confesses that he is that lover, Rosalind/Ganymede questions the depth of his affection, observing that his neat appearance conveys the impression of 'loving yourself than seeming the lover of any other' (3.2.371-2). Later, Rosalind/Ganymede again tests Orlando's sincerity by claiming that were Rosalind and Orlando to marry, Rosalind would cuckold him (commit adultery). Rosalind/Ganymede also challenges Orlando to keep his promise to return at a specified time: 'if you break one jot of your promise or come one minute behind your hour, I will think you the most pathetical break-promise and the most hollow lover and the most unworthy of her you call Rosalind' (4.1.181-4). In short, under cover of her male disguise, Rosalind attempts to determine what kind of husband Orlando will be. Will he be loving, trusting and true? Will he be worthy of her love?

In *The Winter's Tale*, Perdita raises similar concerns about Florizel in the courtship dialogue that opens the play's famous sheep-shearing festival. Their dialogue is fraught with tension over Florizel's sexual intentions and Perdita's discomfort at their discrepancy in status. In reading this dialogue (4.4.1-46), pay attention to the language of wooing as well as of anxiety and resistance. How do Perdita and Florizel address each other? Which specific words provide clues to their feelings, or to important questions of faith, truth or worth? We saw that Rosalind mocks, criticizes and tests Orlando. Do you detect any mockery, criticism or testing in Perdita's words? Pay particular attention to the passage in which Florizel compares himself to the gods of Roman mythology: Jupiter, Neptune and Apollo. How and why is Florizel using mythological allusion here? Are the stories he tells of these figures comedic in genre? Do Perdita and Florizel appear to be using the language of specific genres (words or concepts we might associate with comedy or tragedy) in discussing how their love story might turn out?

The language of comedy II: The combat of wits

Another kind of language that enlivens Shakespearean comedy involves artfully witty, humorous exchanges between men and women. In certain situations, as with Beatrice and Benedick in *Much Ado about Nothing*, men and women tease, debate or insult each other as a kind of prelude to their eventual union in marriage. At other times, a sharp-tongued Clown figure is central to the combat of wits, as with Touchstone in *As You Like It* or Feste in *Twelfth Night*.

One such verbal combat, the initial argument between Petruccio and Katherina in *The Taming of the Shrew*, appears to express some genuine hostility. In this comedy, the wealthy Petruccio arrives in Padua searching for a suitable wife. Having witnessed an exchange between the gentleman Baptista and his two daughters, the fiery Katherina and her younger, more mild sister, Bianca, Petruccio secures Baptista's permission to woo Katherina, despite her apparent disdain for him. In the dialogue below (2.1.181-208), note how each speaker uses language to wrest control of the situation. For instance, despite Katherina's reputation for angry outspokenness, Petruccio perversely praises her as dainty and mild. Their quick exchange of witty, punning, language makes it difficult to draw the line between a joke, a barb and an insult.

PETRUCCIO
  Good morrow, Kate, for that's your name, I hear.
KATHERINA
  Well have you heard, but something hard of hearing:
  They call me Katharine that do talk of me.
PETRUCCIO
  You lie, in faith; for you are called plain Kate
  And bonny Kate, and sometimes 'Kate the Curst'[1];
  But Kate, the prettiest Kate in Christendom,
  Kate of Kate Hall, my super-dainty[2] Kate –
  For dainties[3] are all cates, and therefore 'Kate' –
  Take this of me, Kate of my consolation:
  Hearing thy mildness praised in every town,

---

[1] ill-tempered
[2] very delicate
[3] refined, fancy foods, also called 'cates' (punning on 'Kates')

Thy virtues spoke of and thy beauty sounded[1] –
Yet not so deeply as to thee belongs –
Myself am moved[2] to woo thee for my wife.

KATHERINA
'Moved'. In good time, let him that moved[3] you hither
Re-move you hence. I knew you at the first
You were a moveable[4].

PETRUCCIO
Why, what's a moveable?

KATHERINA
A joint-stool[5].

PETRUCCIO
Thou hast hit it: come, sit on me.

KATHERINA
Asses are made to bear, and so are you.

PETRUCCIO
Women are made to bear[6], and so are you.

KATHERINA
No such jade[7] as you, if me you mean.

PETRUCCIO
Alas, good Kate, I will not burden thee,
For, knowing thee to be but young and light[8] –

KATHERINA
Too light[9] for such a swain as you to catch,
And yet as heavy[10] as my weight should be.

PETRUCCIO
'Should be'?[11] Should – buzz.

KATHERINA
Well ta'en, and like a buzzard[12].

---

[1] proclaimed, punning on 'sounding as taking the sea's depth
[2] incited
[3] brought
[4] piece of furniture
[5] stool made of joined parts
[6] carry the weight of a man (in sex); be pregnant
[7] inferior, worn-out horse
[8] not heavy; frivolous; sexually wanton
[9] swift
[10] weighty, important
[11] punning on 'bee'
[12] predatory bird; stupid person

The trading back and forth of single lines is called 'stichomythia'; we'll discuss this and other rhetorical figures in more depth in Chapter Two. Stichomythia works so well here because it allows each speaker immediately to appropriate, question, mock or twist the other's words. In addition to these rhetorical patterns, note how Katherina and Petruccio refer to food, furniture, animals, birds and insects to describe and insult each other. Humble things from everyday life are appropriate fodder for an argument that takes place in a comedy, which typically brings men and women together to form new domestic units.

It's possible that Shakespeare was recalling this vibrant scene from one of his earliest comedies when he composed the argument between Leontes and Paulina in *The Winter's Tale*. Although the context for the two arguments is very different, Leontes paints Paulina as a kind of 'shrew', or aggressively outspoken woman. Paulina mocks her sovereign as eagerly as Katherina mocks her suitor. It is precisely the tragic context of this combat of wits in *The Winter's Tale* – Leontes's imprisonment of Hermione for adultery and treason – that makes its comic language bristle. When reading the argument between Paulina and Leontes (2.3.65-108), consider how the language used by Paulina and Leontes compares to that used by Katherina and Petruccio, in terms of form, tone and subject matter. In what terms do Paulina and Leontes criticize and insult each other? Do the references to human and animal bodies function similarly or differently in this scene than in the exchange between Katherina and Petruccio? Do you find any witty or humorous language in this passage, despite the seriousness of the matter under dispute? While all that Leontes wants is for Paulina to shut up and leave, Paulina's insistence on engaging in a combat of wits in the face of her sovereign's threats suggests something of the mixed genre of *The Winter's Tale*, in which comedy rubs up against tragedy.

The language of comedy III: Restoration and reunion

We recognize a comedy, generally speaking, as a story that begins in loss, conflict, confusion or suffering and ends in fulfilment, reconciliation, understanding and contentment, at least for some characters. Dante called his epic poem *The Divine Comedy* because it traces the Christian pilgrim's journey from hell to paradise. Shakespearean comedies end with familial reconciliations, betrothals or newly performed marriages, although in some comedies such resolutions are more joyful than in others.

The final scene of *As You Like It* celebrates the reunion of family members, the joining of couples and the upturn of fortune. The revelation that 'Ganymede' was actually Rosalind in male disguise resolves the doubts and confusions caused by the various courtships in which s/he was involved. Rosalind reunites with her father, Duke Senior, who condones her marriage to Orlando. As Rosalind's husband, the previously disenfranchised Orlando thus becomes the heir to the dukedom. Celia will marry Orlando's older brother Oliver. Moreover, Orlando's and Oliver's brother Jacques arrives with the surprising but welcome news that Duke Senior's brother, who had usurped his dukedom, has decided to restore his brother to power. In the following speech (5.4.164-77), Duke Senior acknowledges these comedic restorations:

> Welcome, young man[1].
> Thou offer'st fairly[2] to thy brothers' wedding:
> To one[3] his lands withheld, and to the other[4]
> A land itself at large, a potent dukedom.
> First, in this forest, let us do those ends[5]
> That here were well begun and well begot[6];
> And after, every[7] of this happy number
> That have endured shrewd[8] days and nights with us
> Shall share the good of our returned fortune,
> According to the measure of their states[9].
> Meantime, forget this new-fall'n dignity[10]

---

[1] i.e Jacques, who has just arrived
[2] contribute the good news of the usurping Duke's resignation
[3] Oliver, whose land was confiscated by the usurping Duke
[4] Orlando, who by marrying Rosalind becomes heir to the dukedom that has just been restored to Duke Senior
[5] finish the business
[6] conceived
[7] each one
[8] difficult, trying
[9] according to their social degrees
[10] newly received honor (the return of his dukedom)

And fall into our rustic revelry.
Play, music! And you brides and bridegrooms all,
With measure heaped in joy[1] to th'measures[2] fall.

As the figure of highest 'state' or degree, the Duke uses his authority to pronounce the outcome of the play's events for various characters, with a particular focus on future prosperity and pleasure. At the same time, by recalling the suffering that he and his followers have endured, he suggests that good fortune in love, finances or politics is the reward for those who patiently and virtuously endure hardship. The Duke also directs what his subjects should do now (dance) and what they should do before they return to court (complete the business – presumably of courtship – that was begun in the forest). Note how the repeated word 'measure(s)' imparts a sense of coherent finality to the various events – marriage, dancing, restoration of withheld lands and position – that appropriately conclude a comedy full of 'joy'.

We can look for similar signs of comedic closure in *The Winter's Tale*. When reading the concluding lines of *The Winter's Tale* (5.3.120-55), keep the above passage from *As You Like It* in mind. Which characters use their own authority or appeal to other authority figures to announce the resolution of former conflicts? How are past losses both acknowledged and overwritten? Compared to *As You Like It*, what role does marriage play in the comedic conclusion of *The Winter's Tale*? Are there particular words that signal the emotions or activities you would expect to conclude a comedy?

The Winter's Tale and tragedy

Although *The Winter's Tale* has traits in common with Shakespeare's comedies, it was written in the wake of his major tragedies, such as *Hamlet*, *Othello*, *Macbeth*, *King Lear* and *Anthony and Cleopatra*. Like these plays, *The Winter's Tale* explores extreme psychological

---

[1] with abundant joy
[2] dances

states such as jealousy, paranoia and madness. Also like several of the tragedies, *The Winter's Tale,* along with the three other 'romances', depicts 'the precarious state of rulers who by their absence invite anarchy or by their presumption threaten tyranny' (Jordan 1). Whereas comedies generally begin in sorrow and end in joy, tragedies often begin in relative prosperity, stability or security and end in loss, confusion or destruction. The tragic protagonists in all the aforementioned plays experience a fall from power, a diminishment of happiness and, ultimately, death. Below, we will explore how the language and subjects typical of tragedy inform *The Winter's Tale.*

The language of tragedy I: Counsel and tyranny

In early modern political thought, the tyrant was the antithesis of the good king. Tyrants were kings who usurped the throne and/or ruled wickedly, indulging their passions instead of obeying the laws of the land, ignoring virtuous counsel and disregarding the common good. Macbeth's opponents repeatedly slander him as a tyrant who has murdered to achieve and to maintain his sovereignty. A common sign of tyrannical or absolute rule was the refusal to consult or to heed advisers who might try to curb the monarch's abuse of power. Often, a tyrant will listen only to flatterers, who tell him what he wants to hear for their own political advancement. Macbeth initially seeks the counsel of his friend Banquo, but ultimately becomes the solitary tyrant who makes unilateral decisions intended to preserve his power by whatever means necessary.

Shakespeare depicts the destructive and self-destructive tendencies of tyrannical rule most poignantly in *King Lear*. Lear angrily banishes his loyal daughter Cordelia because he takes her refusal to flatter him as sign of disobedience and cruelty. Lear's chief adviser, the Earl of Kent, interposes to warn the king that he is making a grave mistake, as Cordelia loves Lear more than do her two venal sisters, who didn't hesitate to flatter their father. In the following speech (1.1.140-60), Kent affirms that his duty and love require him to speak the truth, even if the king finds his words insolent and deserving of punishment:

KENT   Royal Lear,
  Whom I have ever honoured as my king,
  Loved as my father, as my master followed,
  As my great patron thought on in my prayers –
LEAR
  The bow is bent and drawn; make from the shaft[1].
KENT
  Let it fall rather, though the fork[2] invade
  The region of my heart: be Kent unmannerly[3]
  When Lear is mad[4]. What wouldst thou do, old man?
  Think'st thou that duty shall have dread[5] to speak,
  When power[6] to flattery bows? To plainness honour's bound,
  When majesty falls to folly. Reserve thy state[7],
  And in thy best consideration check[8]
  This hideous rashness. Answer my life my judgement[9],
  Thy youngest daughter does not love thee least,
  Nor are those empty-hearted, whose low sounds[10]
  Reverb no hollowness[11].
LEAR   Kent, on thy life, no more.
KENT
  My life I never held but as a pawn[12]
  To wage[13] against thy enemies; ne'er fear to lose it,
  Thy safety being the motive.
LEAR   Out of my sight!
KENT
  See better, Lear, and let me still[14] remain
  The true blank[15] of thine eye.

---

[1]avoid the arrow
[2]arrowhead
[3]impolite, rude
[4]insane
[5]fear
[6]i.e. the king
[7]retain your power
[8]restrain
[9]I'll stake my life on my opinion
[10]soft speech
[11]echo no insincerity (e.g. 'hollow' words)
[12]pledge
[13]wager
[14]always
[15]exact bullseye/center

Establishing the 'plainness' or unadorned honesty of his speech against the ornate inventions of flatterers, Kent insists that Lear accept the truth, no matter how difficult it might be for the king to admit that foolish 'rashness' has distorted his judgement. In the face of Lear's threats, Kent explains that since his life is devoted to protecting Lear, he cannot be frightened into silence or servile obedience. Willing to sacrifice everything for his sovereign, Kent boldly asserts that Lear has mistaken honest speech – both Cordelia's and his own – for disloyal speech, and warns of the terrible consequences to follow.

The Winter's Tale contains a tragic catalyst analogous to Lear's banishment of Cordelia. Leontes, believing his wife unfaithful, angrily renounces and imprisons her. As in *King Lear*, Leontes's counsellors intervene, pleading with their sovereign to reconsider his actions. Whereas Kent tries to convince Lear that Cordelia loves him despite her refusal to flatter him, Leontes's counsellors try to convince him that Hermione has not been unfaithful. When reading this passage from *The Winter's Tale* (2.1.126-57), compare the language used by Leontes's counsellors to that used by Kent. What rhetorical strategies do Leontes's counsellors use to convince him that he has made a mistake? What kinds of words and images do they associate with Hermione's innocence? Whereas Kent suggests that Lear does not see the situation clearly, Leontes insists that his senses are sharper than those of his counsellors. What might Leontes mean by this? Does any of the language of this passage hint at the tragedy to come?

The language of tragedy II: Madness and folly

As we saw in Kent's warning to Lear, a counsellor might call his sovereign 'mad' (insane) or foolish to provoke him into reassessing the wisdom of his actions. A staple of Shakespearean tragedy, madness affects Ophelia, Lady Macbeth, King Lear and, at least performatively, Hamlet. Tragic characters like Hamlet or Othello who don't literally go mad from grief or guilt might still suffer mental anguish. Othello's tormented conviction that his wife Desdemona has been unfaithful connects *Othello* with *The Winter's*

Tale; in both plays, jealousy goads the male protagonist into actions that have horrible consequences, including the death of Desdemona and the apparent or actual death of Hermione. In *The Blazon of Jealousy*, a treatise by the Florentine historian Benedetto Varchi that was translated into English in 1615, jealousy is described as a 'strange malady' that causes a 'continual and a perpetual discontentment and disquietness in the mind' (sig. H3r). Jealousy itself is a kind of madness.

We can productively compare the tragic language of jealousy in *Othello* and *The Winter's Tale*. In *Othello*, Iago poisons his master Othello's contentment by convincing him of Desdemona's infidelity. As evidence, Iago manipulates Othello into believing that Desdemona has given her handkerchief to her lover. Othello explains how the love in his heart has been poisoned by the venom of hatred and vengeance: 'Arise, black vengeance, from the hollow hell, / Yield up, O love, thy crown and hearted throne / To tyrannous hate! Swell, bosom, with thy fraught, / For 'tis of aspics' tongues' (3.3.450-3). Othello continues to express his mental torment in impassioned, violent language – 'Damn her, lewd minx: O, damn her, damn her!' (3.3.478) – which climaxes in an incoherent rant when Iago claims that Desdemona's lover has confessed to having had sex with her (4.1.35-43):

> Lie with her? lie on her? We say lie on her, when they belie[1] her! Lie with her, zounds, that's fulsome[2]! – Handkerchief! confessions! handkerchief! – To confess, and be hanged for his labour! First, to be hanged, and then to confess: I tremble at it. Nature would not invest herself in such shadowing passion[3] without some instruction[4]. It is not words[5] that shakes me thus. Pish! Noses, ears, and lips. Is't possible? Confess! handkerchief! O devil!

Note how Othello seems to develop a dialogue with himself by repeating and ringing changes on particular words and phrases, not too unlike the way that we saw Katherina and Petruccio repeating

---

[1] slander
[2] disgusting
[3] My extreme emotional distress would not come so naturally
[4] without a cause (i.e. Desdemona's infidelity)
[5] i.e. it is not words alone

and playing with each other's language. In a comedy, such verbal repetition might increase erotic tension or demonstrate mastery of a courtship situation. In *Othello*, these rhetorical patterns instead signal the extreme anguish and confusion inciting the protagonist to tragic action.

Although *The Winter's Tale* is not (simply) a tragedy, Leontes's language of jealousy is remarkably consonant with Othello's. Just as Othello calls Desdemona a 'lewd minx' and 'devil', Leontes degrades his wife once he believes that she has lost her chastity: 'My wife's a hobby-horse, deserves a name / As rank as any flax-wench that puts to / Before her troth-plight' (1.2.274-6). When Camillo objects that Leontes's words are both vulgar and untrue, Leontes launches into a rant that recalls Othello's broken speech:

LEONTES   Is whispering nothing?
Is leaning cheek to cheek? Is meeting noses?
Kissing with inside lip? Stopping the career
Of laughter with a sigh? – A note infallible
Of breaking honesty. Horsing foot on foot?
Skulking in corners? Wishing clocks more swift?
Hours, minutes? Noon, midnight? And all eyes
Blind with the pin and the web but theirs, theirs only,
That would unseen be wicked? Is this nothing?
Why then the world and all that's in't is nothing,
The covering sky is nothing, Bohemia nothing,
My wife is nothing, nor nothing have these nothings,
If this be nothing.
CAMILLO   Good my lord, be cured
Of this diseased opinion, and betimes,
For 'tis most dangerous.

(1.2.282-96)

As in *Othello*, jealousy is described as a kind of poison or disease. More importantly, consider how Leontes's speech patterns manifest the madness of jealousy in ways comparable to Othello's. What is the effect of repetition in Leontes's speech? What is the particular significance of the word 'nothing'? As in Othello's speech, what is the significance of Leontes's reference to noses and lips – as well as cheeks, feet and eyes? What words or images give this speech a tragic cast, and possibly anticipate the sad events to follow?

Sources, intertexts, allusions

We've considered how Shakespeare's earlier comedies and tragedies function as linguistic and conceptual influences or 'sources' for *The Winter's Tale*. Shakespeare also had a direct source for *The Winter's Tale*: a prose narrative called *Pandosto. The Triumph of Time* (1588) by Robert Greene. Analysing what Shakespeare borrowed and what he also omitted or altered from *Pandosto* can enhance our understanding of the generic hybridity of *The Winter's Tale*. Shakespeare found in Greene's story the major elements for his play: a king who accuses his wife of betraying him with another king, his dear friend; an exiled princess raised by shepherds; a romance between the princess and the son of the second king; the princess' reunion with her father following the revelation of her true identity.

What is the genre of *Pandosto*? The title page of the 1588 edition provides clues to the author's or publisher's understanding of its genre – it's unknown who wrote the 'blurb' advertising the book's contents. Before reading my analysis of the blurb in the next paragraph, identify for yourself any words that might indicate the mood, shape or purpose of the story:

> Wherein is discovered by a pleasant history that although by the means of sinister Fortune Truth may be concealed, yet by Time in spite of Fortune it is most manifestly revealed. Pleasant for age to avoid drowsy thoughts, profitable for youth to eschew other wanton pastimes, and bringing to both a desired content. *Temporis filia veritas.*
>
> (Pitcher 406)

The concluding Latin phrase means 'Truth is the daughter of Time'. Is it possible to determine from this passage if we are about to read a comedy, a tragedy or some other kind of story?

The blurb's definition of *Pandosto* as a 'pleasant history' is not as informative with regard to genre as we might assume, since in sixteenth-century parlance 'history' often simply meant 'narrative', not a chronological account of past events. Despite its seeming blandness, 'pleasant' is a more interesting term here than 'history'. In a famous dictum, the ancient Roman poet Horace declared that poetry had two purposes: to please and to instruct. Praising *Pandosto* as both 'pleasant' and 'profitable', the blurb signals Greene's allegiance to those elevated literary aims. Still, we might suspect that the emphasis on enjoyment in words such as 'pleasant', 'pastimes' and 'content' indicates a comedy. The claim that the story will offer readers a 'desired content' aligns with the fate of lovers in comedy, who usually find the contentment they desired in the form of a betrothal or wedding.

Although the *Pandosto* blurb suggests that 'sinister Fortune' will cause suffering and confusion, it assures us that 'Truth' will eventually be revealed by 'Time'. Hence the concluding motto: 'Truth is the daughter of Time'. A sixteenth-century illustration of this saying portrays Father Time releasing his daughter, Truth, from a dark cave in which she has been imprisoned. As Marion Wells shows, this motto 'came to be associated specifically with the suppression of truth through slander' (247). The blurb thus appears to promise moral 'profit' through a story involving faith in the power of time to discredit slander and reveal truth. That plotline seems to put *Pandosto* on a comic trajectory, in that comedy fundamentally involves a positive turn from frustration to fulfilment, often facilitated by the revelation of a previously occluded truth: in *As You Like It*, 'Ganymede' is revealed to be Rosalind; in *The Winter's Tale*, Perdita is revealed to be the legitimate daughter of Leontes.

In *The Winter's Tale*, Shakespeare borrows from *Pandosto* not only the comedic trajectory of truth vindicated, however, but also the tragic suffering that is hinted at in the blurb's mention of 'sinister Fortune'. At the beginning of *Pandosto*, the narrator, having recounted Pandosto's love for his wife (Bellaria) and son (Garinter), reveals that the king's 'great joy and content' suffer a seemingly arbitrary disaster: 'Fortune, envious of such happy success, willing to show some sign of her inconstancy, turned her wheel and darkened their bright sun of prosperity with the misty clouds of mishap and misery' (Pitcher 407). The image of Fortune turning her wheel derives from the medieval tradition of tragedy known as *de casibus virorum illustrium* ('of the falls of famous men'), in which princes who flourish at the top of Fortune's wheel suddenly descend into misery and death as the wheel cycles downward. Hence, *Pandosto* might be regarded as the tragedy of a king who poisons his own happiness through the 'causeless misery' of jealousy (406).

In the Writing Matters section below, we will consider in more detail the significance of some of the specific changes that Shakespeare makes to *Pandosto*. For now, it will suffice to outline the basic similarities and differences between *Pandosto* and *The Winter's Tale*, with an eye to questions of genre. The most significant change that Shakespeare makes to his source involves Hermione's fate. In *Pandosto*, the news of Garinter's death causes Bellaria to die of grief. Shakespeare follows Greene in having Hermione apparently die of grief from Mamillius's death, but has Hermione return to life after sixteen years: depending on one's interpretation, she is either miraculously revived in the form of a statue or is revealed never to have died in the first place (in the latter case, time reveals the truth of her faked death). Greene also stresses the tragic consequences of Fawnia's return to her father's kingdom before her true identity is discovered. Unaware that Fawnia is his daughter, Pandosto attempts to coerce her into sex. Following the revelation of Fawnia's identity, Pandosto kills himself in a 'great melancholy fit' over the multiple sins he has committed against his family, including his incestuous desire (Pitcher 445). Pandosto's suicide 'close[s] up the comedy' of the marriage between Dorastus and Fawnia 'with a tragical stratagem' (445). In *The Winter's Tale*, Perdita is not subjected to sexual assault, although Diane Purkiss describes the threat of incest as one of the play's 'nightmare worlds which Leontes evades by a hair's breadth' (76). Arguably, the other most important change Shakespeare makes to *Pandosto* is the invention of Paulina. Consider how different *The Winter's Tale* would be without Paulina's defence of Hermione's innocence, defiance of Leontes and orchestration of Hermione's reunion with Perdita and Leontes.

Shakespeare borrowed from Robert Greene not only for the main plot of *The Winter's Tale*, but also for the character of Autolycus. In 1592, Greene published two 'coney-catching' pamphlets detailing the methods used by London con-artists to catch gullible 'conies' (rabbits) in their traps. For instance, a pick-pocket feigns illness in order to rob the kind farmer who stops to help him, and two rogues sing ballads while their partners cut the purses of those who gather to listen. Autolycus uses precisely these tricks first to pick the Clown's pocket and later to cut the purses of rustics distracted by the Clown's singing (4.3.49-116, 4.4.609-23). Some scholars have suggested that Autolycus, a shape-shifting trickster who sells lies and tells tales, represents Robert Greene (Newcomb, *Reading*

123-4; Das 24), or a London actor (Schalkwyk 272-3), or even Shakespeare, whose play is a 'veritable feast of filching' involving the 'open theft' of Greene's and others' work (Baldo 3).

Whereas Greene's texts are direct sources for *The Winter's Tale*, throughout this book we will also explore the play's many indirect sources and intertexts, the latter referring to a literary text that is related to another literary text, often through allusions. Lori Newcomb argues that the allusions to Ethiopia and Libya in *The Winter's Tale* point to an ancient Greek romance, Heliodorus's *Aethiopica* (translated into English in 1569), as an underacknowledged source for the play ('Source' 37; cf. Reynolds). Newcomb argues that because 'stories spread interculturally', we might do well to embrace 'infinite regress, multiplicity, [and] incertainty' instead of the fantasy of an 'original' source ('Source' 34). *Pandosto* 'may be a direct, primary, and visible precursor to *The Winter's Tale*, but it is not its source in the etymological sense, not its point of origin' (Newcomb, 'Source' 34). In addition to the *Aethiopica*, another intercultural 'source' for *The Winter's Tale* is the work of the ancient Roman poet Ovid, who supplies material for the play's allusions to Flora, Proserpina, Jupiter, Neptune and Apollo.

The Proserpina myth is particularly important in supplying a model for the representation of seasonal time in *The Winter's Tale*. During the sheep-shearing festival, Perdita wishes that she had spring flowers such as daffodils and violets to distribute to her young guests: 'O Proserpina, / For the flowers now that, frighted, thou let'st fall / From Dis' wagon!' (4.4.116-18). Proserpina was the virgin daughter of Ceres, goddess of agriculture. One day when Proserpina is gathering flowers in the Sicilian countryside, Dis (or Pluto), god of the dead, abducts her and carries her to the underworld in his chariot. After an appeal from Ceres, Jove, king of the gods and Proserpina's father, decrees that Proserpina will live six months each year in the underworld with her husband, Dis, and the other six in Sicily with her mother. When Proserpina lives in the underworld, the earth is cold and dark (winter); when she lives with her mother, the weather is warm and bright (summer). In *Pandosto*, Pandosto (the Leontes figure) is king of Bohemia and Egistus (the Polixenes figure) is king of Sicily. Shakespeare perhaps reversed these locales in order to have Perdita, like Proserpina, be taken away from and finally returned to her mother in Sicily. How else might the Proserpina myth impact your understanding of Perdita's and Hermione's experiences of loss and reunion?

In addition to reversing Sicily and Bohemia, Shakespeare, as we have seen, changes the names of Greene's characters: Pandosto becomes Leontes, Bellamira becomes Hermione and so on. Shakespeare's use of names other than those he found in *Pandosto* suggests that they might bear some symbolic or thematic meanings drawn from folk, literary or linguistic sources. The animal names 'Leontes' (leo=*lion* [Latin]) and 'Autolycus' (auto=*lone/himself* + lycus=*wolf* [Greek]) derive from medieval beast fables. Although Leontes is a king and Autolycus a poor rogue, what might their names suggest that they have in common? Exiled and stripped of her identity, Perdita (=*the lost one* [Lat.]) is akin to the mysterious princesses of romance. Paulina, who 'redeems' Hermione from death and requires an awakening of 'faith' (5.3.95, 103), recalls the apostle St. Paul, the first codifier of Christian doctrine (Diehl; Martin). Paulina was also the wife of the ancient Roman philosopher Seneca. In early modern English, 'Hermione' is a 'homonym as well as a synonym for "harmony"' (Leimberg 135). Hermione and Polixenes are also possibly linked via the Trojan War, the subject of Homer's epic poem the *Iliad*. The catalyst for the war was the abduction of Helen of Sparta, King Menelaus's wife, by the Trojan prince Paris. In revenge, the Greeks waged a ten-year campaign against Troy that killed many heroes and destroyed the city. Hermione was the daughter of Helen and Menelaus; the name Polixenes resembles Polyxinus, a Greek king who fought in the Trojan War. Do you find any connections between *The Winter's Tale* and the Trojan War farfetched, or do you think that these allusions might add another dimension to the tragic inception of the play?

Amorous Florizel (flos=*flower* [Lat.]) might trace his roots to the classical eclogue or pastoral poem. The sheep-shearing festival in *The Winter's Tale*, during which Florizel first appears, is an extended pastoral episode. The conventions of pastoral poetry include 'idyllic landscape, landscape as a setting for song, an atmosphere of *otium* [leisure], a conscious attention to art and nature, herdsmen as singers', a festive convening of shepherds and an aestheticized, sometimes allegorical, depiction of the simple rustic life (Alpers 22). Constance Jordan argues that the serious 'ethos of pastoral' is the 'common subjection of all men to nature and its generative powers' (136). In *The Winter's Tale*, a similar sentiment is voiced by Paulina in relation to Hermione's infant daughter: 'This child was prisoner to the womb, and is / By law and process of great Nature thence / Freed and enfranchised, not a party to / The anger of the king' (2.2.58-61). Likewise, Perdita elevates 'great creating Nature' above human artifice and subordinates King Polixenes's local political power to nature's universal power: 'The selfsame sun that shines upon his court / Hides not his visage from our cottage, but / Looks on alike' (4.4.88, 449-51). In addition to stressing our 'common subjection' to nature, pastoral often exists in a timeless realm that promises 'restorations like those of vegetation in spring, always perfect, always complete' (Jordan 107). Is there anything about the sheep-shearing festival that feels timeless? What is the significance of Florizel's role as a (seemingly paradoxical) 'courtly pastoralist' (Alpers 204)? Does Florizel seem at home in a pastoral environment? At the end of the play, how do the seasonal restorations implied by the Proserpina myth or the pastoral ideal affect your experience of the restoration of Perdita to her parents?

Through these allusions to ancient Greek and Roman civilizations, Shakespeare sets *The Winter's Tale* in a vaguely defined, semi-mythical past; at the same time, the play seems recognizably early modern in its depiction of courtly politics and rural festivities, as we will discover in Chapter Three's exploration of the play's historical contexts. For now, it's enough to recognize how Shakespeare draws upon multiple kinds of stories from various cultures, periods and traditions: fairy tales, myths, romances, comedies, tragedies, pastorals, ballads, crime pamphlets, New Testament epistles and so on. If these different sources, intertexts and influences don't seem to mesh, that's precisely the point. *The Winter's Tale* exists in an immensely complex web of oblique, contingent and fragmentary connections to past texts, contemporary texts and texts of our own era. It's up to us what to make of these connections.

What, then, can we conclude about the genre of *The Winter's Tale*? What kind of 'old tale' is it? When reading the play, pay attention to the tone or mood of various scenes. Are there passages or scenes that seem largely mournful? satirical? humorous? silly? frightening? uplifting? solemn? How might such moods correlate – or, just as importantly, fail simply to correlate – with dramatic genres such as comedy and tragedy? Ultimately, I hope that you have come away from this discussion with a healthy scepticism about the purity of generic categories. Genres are best understood as flexible sets of conventions that establish horizons of expectation for readers or audiences. We more or less know what to expect when we watch a horror film, romantic comedy or spy thriller. We would be shocked if a psychopath suddenly appeared and began murdering the protagonists of a romantic comedy or if a festive wedding concluded a violent horror movie. Of course, within the general set of expectations established by a genre, all kinds of artistic liberties can be taken. For any cultural artefact, be it *The Winter's Tale* or the comedy/satire/thriller/horror films *Get Out* (2017) and *Parasite* (2019), we might ask where *we* draw the line between different generic categories. What is the point at which *Get Out* or *Parasite* no longer feels like a comedy? When we shift from Sicily to Bohemia in *The Winter's Tale*, how do the tragic events of the first part of the play continue (or not) to impress themselves on our experience of a more comedic world? How much weight do you give the final scenes of the play in your overall experience of *The Winter's Tale* as comic, tragic or tragicomic?

Writing matters

Reading from the details

When discussing fairy tales above, I introduced the *Oxford English Dictionary* [OED], a historical dictionary of the English language that traces the changing meanings and uses of words through time. The *OED* records the earliest known meanings of a word, as well as meanings that become obsolete or newly emerge with time. Because a word might have meant something very different in 1611 than it does today, the *OED* is a crucial resource for understanding Shakespeare's language. For example, in the early seventeenth century the word 'clown' could denote the social status of 'countryman, rustic, or peasant', or the profession of a 'fool or jester' (clown, *n.* 1a, 3a). A dull-witted rustic, the Clown in *The Winter's Tale* matches the first definition. We will get a very misleading impression of the Clown if we think of the bewigged and painted figure of children's parties and horror films. Above, we also considered Leontes's use of the word 'nothing' when condemning his wife's supposed adultery. In early modern England, 'thing' could also refer to 'the genitals' (thing *n.* 11c). Sometimes Shakespeare uses 'thing' more narrowly to signify a penis; hence 'nothing' (nothing) can signify a vagina. Knowing the sexual connotations of 'nothing' adds an important dimension to our understanding of Leontes's jealous rant. We will delve into the *OED* and its uses in more detail in Chapter One.

Ghost stories

In the rest of this chapter, we will consider how to use writing to explore the issues of genre and source discussed above. We begin with ghost stories: the kind of tales told in films like *The Sixth Sense*, *The Others*, *The Shining* or *Poltergeist*. For us, ghost stories usually fall within the genre of horror. Early modern audiences had similar expectations: ghosts were familiar figures in tragedies, particularly in 'revenge tragedies' featuring horrible murders. For instance, Thomas Kyd's *The Spanish Tragedy* (1589) opens with a ghost seeking vengeance on his killers. The ghost of Hamlet's father returns from the dead to demand revenge against his brother, who gruesomely murdered him. Macbeth has Banquo assassinated only to find Banquo's bloody ghost haunting his dinner party.

Unusually for a play that is not a tragedy, *The Winter's Tale* contains three ghost stories, although no ghost actually appears. Mamillius begins to tell his mother a winter's tale of 'sprites and goblins' in a churchyard (2.1.26). Mamillius never gets to tell his ghost story because Leontes bursts in to accuse Hermione of adultery: one sad story is abandoned for the more serious one unfolding before us. Another ghost story comes late in the play, when Leontes imagines that, were he to remarry, Hermione's spirit would repossess her corpse and incite Leontes to murder his current wife. In this fantasy, Hermione's ghost resembles the ghosts of revenge tragedy who return to seek vengeance against those who did them wrong. This ghost is quite unusual, however, since ghosts in early modern culture and drama are overwhelmingly imagined as male (Dolan 221-2).

The longest and most compelling ghost story in the play is delivered by Antigonus as he carries out the banishment of Hermione's infant daughter. Addressing the infant, Antigonus says:

> I have heard, but not believed, the spirits o'th'dead
> May walk again. If such thing be, thy mother
> Appeared to me last night, for ne'er was dream
> So like a waking. To me comes a creature,
> Sometimes her head on one side, some another;
> I never saw a vessel of like sorrow,
> So filled and so becoming. In pure white robes,
> Like very sanctity, she did approach
> My cabin where I lay; thrice bowed before me,
> And, gasping to begin some speech, her eyes
> Became two spouts;
>
> (3.3.15-25)

This 'creature' admonishes Antigonus to name the infant 'Perdita' and to leave her in Bohemia. Concluding that what he has seen is no dream but actually Hermione's ghost, Antigonus conjectures that Hermione's wish to see the infant delivered to Bohemia confirms that Polixenes is indeed its father.

Following are some writing prompts keyed to Antigonus's speech that you can use to explore the significance of ghost stories in defining the genre of *The Winter's Tale*.

1 Antigonus's description of Hermione is an *ekphrasis*: a detailed description meant to bring a visual image alive for the reader. Write an analysis of Antigonus's speech in which you explain what his account of the appearance, behaviour and speech of Hermione's ghost reveals about him, the teller of this ghost story. You might address the following questions in your analysis. What does Antigonus's ekphrastic description of the ghost reveal about his feelings, beliefs, values or assumptions? What is the significance of the details that he mentions? What is the possible significance of what he *doesn't* say about the ghost? How does he feel about what the ghost says to him? Imagine that you were directing a production of *The Winter's Tale* and decided to have Hermione's ghost appear on stage and deliver her speech to Antigonus directly. Would you have the actor playing the ghost look and behave in accordance with Antigonus's account? Why or why not? If not, how would you costume Hermione's ghost and direct her to behave and speak, and why?

2 If you are familiar with *Hamlet,* consider how the Ghost of Hamlet's father casts Hamlet as the protagonist of a revenge tragedy. Rereading the Ghost's long speech to his son (1.5.42-91), look for language that corresponds to the moods and conventions of tragedy (i.e. a fall from prosperity, violence, death, treachery, political upheaval). What does the Ghost look like, how does he behave, what does he tell (or not tell) Hamlet and what does he want from Hamlet? How does Hamlet respond to this encounter? Now write an analysis of Antigonus's speech in which you explain whether or not his language casts this ghost story in tragic terms. You might address the following questions in your analysis. Does Antigonus's language correspond to the moods and conventions of tragedy? Is it significant that Antigonus is addressing this ghost story to the infant Perdita? According to Antigonus, what does Hermione's ghost look like, how does she behave, what does she tell (or not tell) him and what does she want from him? How does Antigonus respond to this encounter? Does Hermione's ghost bear any resemblance to the vengeful ghosts of revenge tragedy, such as the Ghost in *Hamlet*?

Language and genre: Comedy

In the following sections, you will have the opportunity to write about the way that *The Winter's Tale* uses the kinds of language typically found in comedies, tragedies and romances. Above, we looked at the comedic combat of wits in scenes from *The Taming of the Shrew* and *The Winter's Tale*. It is possible to read the initial dialogue between Hermione and Polixenes (1.2.34-60) as another instance of witty banter between a man and a woman. Following is a writing prompt keyed to this passage that you can use to explore the language of comedy in *The Winter's Tale*. Reread the arguments between Katherina and Petruccio (*TS* 2.1.181-208) and between Paulina and Leontes (*WT* 2.3.65-108), paying attention to tone (e.g. playful, bitter, teasing, aggressive, angry), figurative language (e.g. puns, metaphors) and formal elements (e.g. repeated words, sentence length). Then write an analysis in which you explain how approaching the exchange between Hermione and Polixenes as a comedic battle of wits might illuminate the combativeness as well as the politeness that characterizes courtly language. You might address the following questions in your analysis. What language in this passage conveys a tone of light-hearted wit, humour or playfulness that we would expect of lovers' banter in a comedy? How does the back-and-forth exchange typical of the combat of wits work in this passage? Ultimately, does their dialogue help to explain why Leontes suspects that his wife and friend are secretly lovers?

Language and genre: Tragedy

As we have seen, the idea that monarchs require honest counsel is central to Shakespeare's tragedies as well as to *The Winter's Tale*. Camillo, Antigonus, Paulina and various Lords all attempt to convince Leontes that he will regret the consequences of his jealousy. When the play returns to Sicily in Act Five the role of counsel is still an active question. This time, the problem is not that the monarch ridicules or threatens his counsellors for speaking the unwelcome truth, but that the counsellors disagree over the right course of action. Whereas Paulina exhorts Leontes to honor Hermione's memory by remaining unmarried, Cleomenes and Dion urge him to find a new wife. Following is a writing prompt keyed to this dialogue (5.1.13-52) that you can use to explore the language of tragedy in *The Winter's Tale*.

Reread the passages in which the Earl of Kent warns King Lear of his folly in banishing Cordelia (*KL* 1.1.140-60), and in which Antigonus and a Lord defend Hermione from Leontes's accusations (*WT* 2.1.126-99). Pay attention to the strategies that these counsellors use to persuade their king, and to each king's response. Then write an analysis in which you explain the difference of opinion between Paulina and the other counsellors regarding Leontes's remarriage (*WT* 5.1.13-52). You might address some of the following questions in your analysis. Why does Paulina say that Leontes 'killed' Hermione? How do Leontes and Cleomenes respond to that charge? What reasons does Dion provide in favour of remarriage? How do both Dion and Paulina appeal to religion in making their arguments? How does Paulina refute Dion's advice? What reasons does Leontes give for accepting Paulina's advice instead of Dion's? How does the language of this passage evoke the conventional subjects of both comedy and tragedy?

Language and genre: Romance

In surveying the variety of 'old tale[s]' within *The Winter's Tale*, we noted that Perdita's return to Sicily generates a tragicomic clash of joyous and sorrowful feelings (5.2.46). The wonder surrounding Perdita's return – and then Hermione's return – is a sign that we are in the world of romance, where strange events bring unexpected closure to stories of suffering and loss. Not surprisingly, 'wonder' appears seven times in *The Winter's Tale*: once in Act Three, once in Act Four, and five times in Act Five. Of the three other plays usually designated as romances, 'wonder' appears seven times each in *Cymbeline* and *The Tempest* and six times in *Pericles*. Wonder, which one critic describes as the 'shocked limit of feeling', seems by definition to thwart linguistic expression (Cunningham 92). Of Perdita's return, one courtly observer says, 'I never heard of such another encounter, which lames report to follow it and undoes description to do it' (5.2.55-7). Theatre audiences might experience wonder, according to Tom Bishop, as an 'intense emotive response' in which 'categorical boundaries dissolve' (3). Wonder thus 'registers not the audience's analysis of the action, but something more like their sense of its significance. Wonder... is less directed to the acquisition of knowledge than to the perception of meaning' (Bishop 4). The following writing exercise offers an opportunity to explore how the implausible events of romance might generate the 'notable passion of wonder' for characters and audience members alike (5.2.12).

First, choose *one* of the following three passages in which the Gentleman and the Steward describe the court's reaction to the discovery of Perdita's identity: 5.2.8-19, 5.2.41-57 or 5.2.68-79. Then, in a paragraph or two, analyse how the passage you selected represents the emotional experience of wonder as a mixture of joy and sorrow. You might consider addressing the following questions in your analysis. How does wonder manifest in the bodies of those affected by it? What is the effect of a storyteller claiming that it is impossible to tell the story he is telling? How might the antithetical feelings that comprise wonder be illuminated by the monologue of

Time, who reigns over 'both joy and terror, / Of good and bad, that makes and unfolds error' (4.1.1-2)? What does the passing of time have to do with the feeling of wonder? What is redeemable and what is irredeemable from the 'wide gap' of sixteen years that has divided the terrible loss from the joyful return of Perdita (4.1.7)?

Working with sources

This section offers an opportunity to use writing to explore Shakespeare's transformations of his primary source, Greene's *Pandosto*. As we have seen, in *The Winter's Tale* Shakespeare borrows from multiple literary sources and traditions, creating a hybrid drama that combines elements of comedy and tragedy. Of course, a major difference between *Pandosto* and *The Winter's Tale* is that the former is a prose narrative and the latter is a play. Choral figures such as Time are the closest that Shakespearean drama gets to a narrator who can provide information unavailable to any particular character. In a prose text such as *Pandosto*, a narrator might not only offer a global perspective on past and present actions, but might also reveal what characters are thinking. The differences between unmediated dialogue in drama and mediated accounts of what characters are doing and thinking in prose narrative will be important in addressing the differences between *The Winter's Tale* and *Pandosto*.

This writing exercise concerns the representation in each text of the tragic onset of the king's jealousy. In *Pandosto*, the narrator recounts how the growing but 'honest familiarity' (chaste intimacy) between Bellaria and Egistus, King of Sicilia, sparks Pandosto's suspicions. In *The Winter's Tale*, Leontes first reveals his suspicions when Hermione, having convinced Polixenes to extend his visit, accompanies him into the garden. Paying attention to particular words, images or metaphors in both texts, first write a paragraph analysing the onset of Pandosto's jealousy (in the passage reproduced below); then write a paragraph analysing Shakespeare's transformation of his source material in the corresponding scene (*WT* 1.2.108-20). You might want to address the following issues in your analysis. In each text, what is the 'evidence' of the supposed adultery? How certain are we that the king's suspicions of adultery are unjustified? How rational or irrational does the king appear to be when collecting evidence and drawing conclusions from that evidence? Do you find either Pandosto or Leontes sympathetic in the belief that he has been betrayed by his wife and friend?

From *Pandosto*:

This honest familiarity increased daily more and more between them, for Bellaria noting in Egistus a princely and bounteous mind, adorned with sundry and excellent qualities, and Egistus finding in her a virtuous and courteous disposition, there grew such a secret uniting of their affections that the one could not well be without the company of the other, insomuch that, when Pandosto was busied with such urgent affairs that he could not be present with his friend Egistus, Bellaria would walk with him into the garden, where they two in private and pleasant devices would pass away the time to both their contents. This custom still continuing betwixt them, a certain melancholy passion entertaining the mind of Pandosto drove him into sundry and doubtful thoughts. First he called to mind the beauty of his wife Bellaria, the comeliness and bravery of his friend Egistus, thinking that love was above all laws, and therefore to be stayed with no law; that it was hard to put fire and flax together without burning; that their open pleasures might breed his secret displeasures. He considered with himself that Egistus was a man and must needs love; that his wife was a woman and therefore subject unto love, and that where fancy forced, friendship was of no force.

(Pitcher 408)

The following exercise addresses the depiction of the princess's return to her homeland in *Pandosto* and *The Winter's Tale*, just prior to the revelation of her true identity. When Dorastus (claiming to be one 'Meleagrus') and Fawnia arrive in Pandosto's kingdom, Pandosto imprisons Dorastus and attempts to seduce Fawnia. Paying attention to particular words, images or metaphors in both texts, first write a paragraph analysing how Pandosto's treatment of Fawnia affects the tone near the conclusion of *Pandosto* (in the passage reproduced below); then write a paragraph analysing how Shakespeare transforms his source material in the corresponding scene (*WT* 5.1.203-31). You might want to address the following issues in your analysis. How does the spectre of tragedy intrude into both episodes? How does each passage address the problem of marriage between a commoner and a prince? How does each writer represent the problem of an older man's attraction to a much younger woman (who happens to be his daughter)? What is the significance of Perdita's silence and Paulina's intervention in this passage? How would you describe the tone or mood at the end of Shakespeare's scene?

From *Pandosto*:

But again to Pandosto who, broiling at the heat of unlawful lust, could take no rest, but still felt his mind disquieted with his new love, so that his nobles and subjects marvelled greatly at this sudden alteration, not being able to conjecture the cause of this his continued care. [Fawnia rejects Pandosto's sexual advances]. Pandosto, seeing that there was in Fawnia a determinate courage to love Meleagrus, and a resolution without fear to hate him, flung away from her in a rage, swearing if in short time she would not be won with reason, he would forget all courtesy and compel her to grant by rigor. But these threatening words no whit dismayed Fawnia but that she still both despited and despised Pandosto. [Egistus arrives, reveals that Meleagrus is his son Dorastus, and asks that Fawnia be put to death. Pandosto conveys his sentence to Fawnia].

Thou disdainful vassal, thou currish kite, assigned by the Destinies to base fortune and yet with an aspiring mind gazing after honour. How durst thou presume, being a beggar, to match with a prince; by thy alluring looks to enchant the son of a king to leave his own country to fulfil thy disordinate lusts? O despiteful mind! A proud heart in a beggar is not unlike to a great fire in a small cottage, which warmeth not the house but burneth it. Assure thyself thou shalt die;

(Pitcher 443)

Keeping a reading journal

This final section outlines the benefits of keeping a journal as you read *The Winter's Tale* (or any Shakespeare play). You can start by following these guidelines until you are experienced enough to make whatever modifications best suit your needs:

1. While reading the play, whenever you come across a particularly intriguing or difficult passage (up to about 20 lines), write out the passage on the left side of a notebook in black ink.

2. Next, use different colour pens (if you choose) to mark up the passage: circle any formal patterns (e.g. rhymes, related words such as 'grace' and 'gracious', parallel structures); draw lines connecting repeated words; underline important phrases or rhetorical figures; put an asterisk by any words or phrases that need to be looked up in the *OED* or that would repay closer analysis, and so on.

3. Then, building from these observations, spend a few minutes annotating the passage. You might explicate metaphors, define words, paraphrase difficult lines, comment on the significance of particular images, record allusions and so on.

4. Finally, on the right page of the notebook, use what you have learned from your annotation to write a brief interpretative comment about the passage. How does your analysis of words, rhetoric and imagery lead you to an interpretation of the significance of this passage? What does the language of this passage reveal about the character(s) speaking? How does the language of this passage connect it to other passages or thematic concerns in the play?

Customize this task as you see fit: some people, for instance, like to use one colour pen to mark words to look up, another colour to underline figures of speech, another colour to connect repeated words and so on. While this exercise might at first seem tedious, reading actively is an extremely good habit that pays off in the long run. Moreover, your annotations and comments will provide a wealth of material to return to when formulating a paper topic or collecting textual evidence for an argument. If you become intrigued with a particular issue in the play, such as the limitations of monarchical authority, you might choose to record and annotate primarily those passages that address that issue. After a few journal entries, you will have a helpful archive of textual evidence and will be able to detect significant patterns in both the play (such as repeated keywords) and your own thinking about the topic.

1

Engaging the language of the text(s)

The texts of *The Winter's Tale*

Before embarking upon a serious examination of Shakespeare's language, we need to understand that modern editions (such as the one you are using) are not accurate reproductions of the plays as they were written, performed and published in Shakespeare's time. When editing texts that were first published in the sixteenth or seventeenth century, scholars make several modifications. They correct evident printing errors that might confuse us; regularize speech prefixes so that we know who is speaking (e.g. King Richard's lines will be prefaced by *Richard* throughout the play, instead of alternating between *Rich.* and *King*); add stage directions that help us to imagine actions or sounds in performance; indicate asides (lines that characters speak to themselves, out of the hearing of other characters) so that we understand how characters are interacting on stage; update obsolete or inconsistent spellings so that we can more easily recognize words; and alter punctuation so that we are not misled by obsolete grammatical conventions. Editors do all these things for the very good reason of making four-hundred-year-old texts more accessible to today's readers. Some of these changes, however, can make it more difficult for us to access potentially meaningful details that appeared in the original published texts.

For instance, the early texts of *The Merchant of Venice* use different speech prefixes for Shylock, the Jewish usurer who is treated contemptuously in Christian Venice: sometimes he is *Shy.*, and sometimes *Jew*. While the writers and printers of early modern texts were not as concerned with internal consistency as we are, the identification of this character as *Jew* suggests that Shakespeare (or whoever prepared his manuscript for publication) placed significant emphasis on the kind of difference represented by a Jew living in a Christian polity – a difference explicitly marked in the play when Shylock is identified as an 'alien' (non-citizen) in Venice (4.1.344). Alternatively, if the speech prefix *Jew* means to indicate that Shylock is a 'typical' (and wicked) representative of his faith, the prejudice encoded in the printed text of the play would thus mirror the prejudice expressed by the Christians within the play (Drakakis). So as not to reproduce an offensive sixteenth-century prejudice, every modern editor of *The Merchant of Venice* regularizes this speech prefix to *Shylock*. Through this reasonable accommodation to modern sensibilities, readers lose whatever insight the original presence of the *Jew* speech prefix might provide into the religious and ethnic politics of the play and of Shakespeare's culture.

Because every editor makes their own choices about how to modernize an early text, no two editions will produce exactly the same 'Shakespeare'. Editors also typically include interpretative aids such as glosses (explanations of words or lines), literary references, historical contexts, discursive notes, accounts of scholarly debates etc., that shape our perspectives on what we are reading. To further complicate matters, some of Shakespeare's plays exist in more than one early printed version; when these early texts vary significantly from each other, editors must decide which version they will use as the basis of their own edition. For instance, the 1623 publication of *King Lear* differs in important respects from the 1608 publication of *King Lear*. Hence modern editors of *King Lear* print *either* the 1608 or the 1623 text; offer *both* texts as two distinct versions of the play; or fashion a *hybrid* text that takes elements from both early texts, thus presenting a 'conflated' text that was never published in that form during the seventeenth century (Mowat, 'Facts').

Unlike *King Lear*, *The Winter's Tale* does not have a complex early publishing history. The two main formats in which Shakespeare's plays were published during the sixteenth and seventeenth centuries are the quarto and the folio, terms that refer to the size of paper used in manufacturing the book. 'Folio' refers to a full-size sheet of paper folded once to make two leaves (or four pages) in a book. Since this sheet of paper was folded only once, the resulting pages are quite large. For a quarto, a full-size sheet of paper was folded twice to make four leaves (or eight pages); since the paper was folded twice, the resulting pages are smaller. A quarto was a small, relatively inexpensive book, the early modern equivalent of a paperback. Folios, by contrast, were large and very expensive; they were usually reserved for collections of significant poetic, philosophical, theological or historical texts. In 1623, several years after Shakespeare's death, members of his acting company compiled thirty-six of his plays into a folio edition titled *Mr. William Shakespeare's Comedies, Histories, and Tragedies*. Today, this book is simply called the 'First Folio', since revised editions of the collection were later published in 1632 (the 'Second Folio'), 1663 (the 'Third Folio') and 1685 (the 'Fourth Folio'). The First Folio is considered a landmark book because it was the first time that a folio comprised entirely of contemporary English plays was published in England. The First Folio was a risky financial endeavour, as a 'large, expensive volume of plays was not guaranteed to sell well, and whatever profits might eventually come were certain to be delayed for many months after the initial investment' (Kastan 63).

Because *The Winter's Tale* was not published in quarto form, the earliest authoritative text of the play that we have appears in the First Folio. The actors who collected and published Shakespeare's plays in the First Folio made their own editorial interventions, some of which are doubtless invisible to us, which is not surprising considering the collaborative efforts that went into writing and publishing plays at the time. As David Scott Kastan explains, 'Shakespeare has become virtually the iconic name for authorship itself, but he wrote in circumstances in which his individual achievement was inevitably dispersed into – if not compromised by – the collaborations necessary for both play and book production' (16). Gary Taylor estimates that 'anywhere from a quarter to a third of Shakespeare's plays contain material written by other professional playwrights' (141), including *Pericles*, *Henry VIII*, *The Two Noble Kinsmen*, *Macbeth* and probably *1 Henry VI*, *Titus Andronicus*, *Edward III* and *Sir Thomas More* (Jowett 106). Although we tend to stress Shakespeare's originality, Taylor describes the drama of Shakespeare and his contemporaries as 'an expression of "artiginality": the creativity of artisans who tinker with inherited forms and stories' (146). Shakespeare displayed 'artiginality' in adapting Greene's *Pandosto* and many other kinds of stories for *The Winter's Tale*. After his death, members of his company, including his erstwhile collaborator John Fletcher, revised, reshaped and edited his texts for both performance and publication (Kastan 68).

One possible intervention that Shakespeare's company made while preparing the First Folio was the division of plays into five acts, since it's unlikely that Shakespeare composed his plays with that structure in mind. By dividing the plays into five acts and marking those divisions with Latin text – so that '*Actus primus, Scena prima*' stands for 'Act one, Scene one' – the compilers of the First Folio presented Shakespeare's plays as authoritative 'classical' texts, comparable to the plays of the ancient Roman writers Terence and Seneca (*Hamlet on the Ramparts*). Although modern editors of *The Winter's Tale* follow the lead of the Folio and of subsequent eighteenth-century editors in dividing the play into five acts, that division might occlude the organic structure of the play. Once you eliminate the imposition of a five-act structure, it's easy to see *The Winter's Tale* as a three-act play in which each act roughly aligns with the different generic categories we discussed in the Introduction. The first act of the play, including the banishment of Perdita and the deaths of Mamillius, Antigonus and Hermione, constitutes a tragedy. The second act of the play is a pastoral comedy focused on Perdita and Florizel in Bohemia. The third and final act, which returns to Sicily, provides the romance or tragicomic ending.

Listening to the language of the opening scene

A significant difference between the First Folio and modern Shakespeare editions concerns the amount of information that modern editors provide even before we start reading the play. Modern editions typically include an introduction, a list of characters – sometimes with detailed notes about each character – and an indication of the setting. *The Winter's Tale* is among just a handful of plays in the First Folio that contain a list of characters. Yet since those lists, with one exception, are printed at the end of the plays, their evident intention is not to give readers information to help orient them during a first reading of the text. Seventeenth-century readers, just like theatre audiences, would have simply relied on the words spoken by characters to orient themselves at the beginning of a play.

What can the opening dialogue of *The Winter's Tale* tell us? A character identified in the First Folio speech prefixes as Archidamus (but never named in the dialogue) provides an initial glimpse into matters of location, social status and unfolding events: 'If you shall chance, Camillo, to visit Bohemia on the like occasion whereon my services are now on foot, you shall see, as I have said, great difference betwixt our Bohemia and your Sicilia' (1.1.1-4). We can infer from this that Archidamus comes from Bohemia ('our Bohemia') and Camillo from Sicily ('your Sicilia'). Both characters are 'now' in Sicily, where Archidamus is performing 'services'; Camillo might in the future visit Bohemia on a 'like occasion'. Camillo's response indicates that these 'services' and 'visits' concern their respective monarchs: 'I think this coming summer the King of Sicilia means to pay Bohemia the visitation which he justly owes him' (1.1.5-7). Since Archidamus and Camillo seem well aware of the diplomatic schedules of their kings, seventeenth-century playgoers or readers would probably have identified them as courtiers. Moreover, they speak the refined language of diplomacy. Archidamus compliments Camillo by admitting that the Bohemians will be unable to match the opulent 'entertainment' provided by the Sicilians. In the following dialogue, observe how the speakers are not exchanging information as much as they are performing courtly compliment:

ARCHIDAMUS
Wherein our entertainment shall shame us, we will be justified in our loves; for indeed –
CAMILLO
Beseech you –
ARCHIDAMUS
Verily, I speak it in the freedom of my knowledge. We cannot with such magnificence – in so rare – I know not what to say.
(1.1.8-13)

Even with these small words ('indeed', 'Beseech you', 'Verily') the speakers demonstrate an eagerness to please. As we will discuss later, the failure of language to communicate truth is a major theme in *The Winter's Tale*. For now, we might observe that Archidamus introduces this theme by declaring his inability to express his feelings about his nation's inferior hospitality. How might this confessed failure of language itself comprise a performance of courtliness? What might Archidamus have to gain from such a confession?

Archidamus and Camillo also provide two crucial pieces of information that will colour our experience of the following scene, in which we meet the aforementioned kings of Bohemia and Sicily. First, Camillo rehearses the kings' long-standing 'affection' – an important word repeated throughout the play, as we will see later (1.1.24). Although separated by their familial and political duties, the kings have maintained their 'loves' over the years through letters, gifts and 'loving embassies', and have figuratively 'embraced as it were from the ends of opposed winds' (1.1.28, 30-1). Camillo's language establishes the intimate, lasting relationship between the kings that shockingly unravels in the following scene. Archidamus and Camillo also relay that the Sicilian king's 'young prince, Mamillius', holds 'great promise' as the future king, and as such 'physics the subject' or gives new life to the Sicilian people (1.1.34, 38-9). The courtiers say nothing, however, about the king's wife, Hermione, or her pregnancy. What does their focus on Mamillius convey about the world of the play? How does this brief scene provide an important context for the impending tragedy of Mamillius's death? We might also observe that though it is generally true that Shakespeare's aristocratic characters speak in the more 'elevated' style of verse, Archidamus and Camillo speak in prose throughout this scene. Why might prose be a fitting medium for this conversation?

When I asked above what the focus on Mamillius's future promise might reveal about the world of the play, I meant to refer broadly to the values or ethos of the society depicted in *The Winter's Tale*. In addition to that broad perspective, it is also productive to consider more specifically what the text reveals or does not reveal about the time(s) and place(s) in which the play is set. Aside from naming the monarchies of Bohemia and Sicily, the opening scene tells us little about these places or about the epoch in which the play occurs. London theatre companies generally did not use scenery or historically accurate costumes that would allow an audience visually to place a play in a particular country or time period; an actor would have worn contemporary finery whether he was portraying a fifteenth-century English king, as in Shakespeare's *Henry V*, or a sixteenth-century Venetian duke, as in *Othello*. Especially with comedies and tragicomedies, even when a play is set in a particular place, such as the Vienna of *Measure for Measure*, Shakespeare shows little concern for historically accurate detail. Hence the locales in *The Winter's Tale* have little relation to the seventeenth-century political or cultural situations of Sicily, a Catholic state ruled by Spain, or Bohemia, a Protestant state ruled by Austria.

In the second scene of the play, characters of royal status allude to Christian concepts such as heaven, original sin, grace and devils that were central to religious belief in early modern Europe (1.2.73-5, 80, 82). From the details provided in these first two scenes, we might deduce that *The Winter's Tale* depicts a medieval or early modern European court. It thus might come as a surprise when Leontes dispatches an embassy to 'sacred Delphos, to Apollo's temple' in order to consult an 'oracle' (2.1.183, 185). This reference to ancient Greek mythology is our first clue that the play takes place in the pagan (pre-Christian) world of classical antiquity. Shakespeare does not attempt to create any kind of historical authenticity for this world. Nonetheless, it is worth pondering the effects of the apparent misalignment between the play's references to Christian theology and its explicitly pre-Christian setting.

Editorial interventions: Spelling, capitalization, punctuation

By paying attention to what characters say, we can usually glean all the contextual information we need for basic comprehension without recourse to a modern editor's notes. In this fundamental way, modern editions do not improve significantly on early printed editions such as the First Folio. It is important, however, to be aware of the changes that modern editors make to the texts of early printed editions. Let's compare a short passage from the First Folio *Winter's Tale* to the same passage in the modern Arden Shakespeare volume edited by John Pitcher. In this passage (reproduced below first from Pitcher's edition and then from the First Folio), Leontes observes that the tenderness of human nature sometimes reveals itself in ways that hard-hearted people find ridiculous:

> How sometimes nature will betray its folly,
> Its tenderness, and make itself a pastime
> To harder bosoms. Looking on the lines
> Of my boy's face, methoughts I did recoil
> Twenty-three years, and saw myself unbreeched,
> In my green velvet coat;
> (Pitcher ed., 1.2.151-6)

> How sometimes Nature will betray it's folly?
> It's tendernesse? and make it selfe a Pastime
> To harder bosomes? Looking on the Lynes
> Of my Boyes face, me thoughts I did requoyle
> Twentie three yeeres, and saw my selfe vn-breech'd,
> In my greene Veluet Coat;
> (First Folio)

Contemplating his son's face, Leontes imaginatively travels twenty-three years back in time to his own childhood, before he was 'breeched'. In early modern England, elite boys wore long coats and were tended by women (as we see with Mamillius in 2.1) until about age eight, when they were 'breeched' – dressed in breeches (knee-length trousers) – and placed in the care of male tutors. In the First Folio text, notice the capitalized words 'Nature', 'Pastime', 'Lynes', 'Boyes' and 'Veluet Coat'. Are these words particularly significant? Are there any non-capitalized words that seem equally important? What changes does Pitcher make to the Folio text, and how do those changes affect your understanding of the passage? Consider what the question marks removed by Pitcher might convey about Leontes's state of mind as he speaks those first three lines. Could an actor deliver these lines in a way that conveyed whatever feelings might be suggested by the question marks?

When comparing an early text to a modern edition, you will always find changes to spelling, capitalization and punctuation. Shakespeare wrote in an era before the advent of standardized spelling, in which each word has (usually) a single 'correct' spelling, and this correct spelling is authorized by a dictionary. According to Russ McDonald, lack of standardization is 'the most notable feature of the English language in the last half of the sixteenth century' (*Arts* 17). The word 'years', for instance, might have been spelled 'yeeres', 'yeares' or 'years'. This doesn't mean, of course, that a writer could spell a word however they wished. Shakespeare couldn't write 'cheenghe' and expect anyone to know that he meant 'king'. Nonetheless, there was no single authority to dictate correct spelling, which was instead 'governed by such various determinants as sound, etymology, whim, and the physical requirements of the printing house' (McDonald, *Arts* 17).

Early modern texts also capitalize or italicize words in seemingly random ways. Some scholars and actors argue that such typographical indications in the First Folio record the performance practices of Shakespeare's company. According to this theory, when a word is capitalized in the First Folio, it means that an actor would have stressed that word to convey its thematic or imagistic significance. Similarly, it has been argued, the First Folio italicizes character names because speaking names emphatically during a performance would help an audience keep track of who was who on stage (Reinhart). Punctuation is generally sparser in the First Folio than in modern editions because early modern actors generally delivered lines quickly: too many commas or periods would have slowed down their pace. As Abigail Rokison observes, in early modern grammars the 'perceived function of punctuation' is as 'a guide to breathing and pausing when reading or speaking a text aloud' (288-9). In other words, punctuation in early modern texts tends to function more rhetorically – with commas indicating short pauses and periods long pauses – than grammatically.

As a final illustration of editorial intervention, let's look at the First Folio text of Leontes's notoriously difficult 'Can thy dam?' speech (1.2.137-46), and then at Pitcher's alterations to it. With such a challenging passage, it's helpful to paraphrase, or put it in your own words Below I have quoted the Folio text of the speech, followed by my own paraphrase. Mine is just one possible paraphrase of the meaning of this highly ambiguous passage. In this monologue, Leontes agonizingly ponders whether or not his suspicions of Hermione's adultery are true. He begins the monologue by addressing to Mamillius his concerns about the possibility that Mamillius's mother (his 'Dam') has betrayed him:

Can thy Dam, may't be
Affection? thy Intention stabs the Center.
Thou do'st make possible things not so held,
Communicat'st with Dreams (how can this be?)
With what's vnreall: thou coactive art,
And fellow'st nothing. Then 'tis very credent,
Thou may'st co-ioyne with something, and thou do'st,
(And that beyond Commission) and I find it,
(And that to the infection of my Braines,
And hardning of my Browes.)

                                              (First Folio)

Leontes asks if it is possible that Hermione has betrayed him ('Can thy Dam' [have committed adultery]?) out of sexual 'Affection' (a word that could refer to any strong feeling) for Polixenes. At the same time, Leontes seems to wonder if his own emotional turbulence ('may't be / [my own] Affection?') has led him to suspect Hermione unjustly. His strong emotion, which intensively pierces him to the core ('thy Intention stabs the Center'), might have generated fantasies of betrayal that do not correspond to reality (since such fantasies 'Communicat[e] with Dreams' and with 'what's vnreall'). Is Hermione really unfaithful or is Leontes dreaming ('how can this be')? Although his anguished suspicions might have arisen from 'nothing' (and thus be false), they might also have arisen from 'something' that actually happened (and thus be true). Leontes concludes with confidence ('Then 'tis very credent') that his suspicions have been generated in response to or connection with Hermione's adultery ('Thou [my jealous feelings] may'st co-ioyne with something, and thou do'st'). He defines adultery here as a behaviour that exceeds what is allowed by his patriarchal authority ('And that beyond Commission'). Leontes's certainty about Hermione's betrayal ('I find it' [to be true]) is evidenced by the poisoning of his mind ('the infection of my Braines') and by the conventional growth of cuckold's horns on his forehead ('the hardning of my Browes'). In early modern folk belief, a cuckold – a husband whose wife has been unfaithful – sprouted horns on his forehead that would reveal his sexual humiliation.

When reading Pitcher's version of the monologue below, look for the kinds of alterations to spelling, punctuation and capitalization that we examined earlier:

> Can thy dam? May't be
> Affection? – Thy intention stabs the centre,
> Thou dost make possible things not so held,
> Communicat'st with dreams – how can this be? –
> With what's unreal thou coactive art,
> And fellow'st nothing. Then 'tis very credent
> Thou mayst co-join with something, and thou dost,
> And that beyond commission, and I find it,
> And that to the infection of my brains
> And hard'ning of my brows.
>
> (Pitcher 1.2.137-46)

Do any of Pitcher's emendations make the passage easier to understand? Why or why not? Does Pitcher's modernization of capitalization and punctuation obscure any indications as to what Leontes might be thinking or feeling?

When reading Shakespeare, it is rewarding to consider different possible meanings of the same word or line(s) in order to generate more than one plausible interpretation. For instance, what if Leontes when describing the destructive intensity of 'affection' is identifying 'as the cause of his torture his own passionate love for his wife, the very basis of romantic marriage' (Belsey, *Eden* 107)? Can you identify lines in his speech in which Leontes might be wondering if his affection for Hermione is the force that both brings them together and tears them apart? Alternatively, what if we were to understand 'affection' as referring not (or not primarily) to Leontes's feelings but to Hermione's? If Leontes's foremost concern is not 'psychological self-diagnosis' but Hermione's sexual attraction to Polixenes, we might look for evidence in the speech of his anxiety about sexual betrayal (Ward 552). Where does Leontes's language possibly evoke the imagery of illegitimate coupling?

Finally, let's consider the more radical editorial intervention performed on the same passage in the No Fear Shakespeare series, which provides 'translations' of Shakespeare into modern English. Having reread Pitcher's version of Leontes's speech, compare the No Fear translation below:

> Can your mother have? Could it be?
> Jealousy's intensity strikes me through to my
> heart and makes things that are impossible

seem possible. That jealousy speaks in
dreams. How can this be? It collaborates
with what's unreal and corresponds to
nothing in real life. Then it's very believable
that my jealousy may be real, and she's
gone beyond what's permitted, and I would
find out and grow insane, and my brow
would harden into horns.

(SparkNotes Editors)

How does the No Fear translation clarify the possible meaning of particular words, clear up ambiguities or resolve difficulties of syntax? Though comprehension is generally a virtue, the No Fear translation also has its downsides. In the First Folio passage, Leontes begins speaking to Mamillius and then shifts to a personified Affection, using the familiar forms of the second person pronoun ('thy' intention, 'thou' dost, 'thou' coactive art). What nuances of meaning might be lost when the SparkNotes editors have Leontes use the third person ('jealousy's intensity', 'jealousy speaks', 'it collaborates') instead of speaking directly to Affection?

The No Fear version also removes the ambiguous meaning(s) of 'affection' by translating that word as 'jealousy'. How might the reduction of 'affection' to 'jealousy' close down some possible meanings for Leontes's monologue? Shakespeare tends to weave patterns of words or images throughout a play, thus linking characters, events and ideas in complex and sometimes unexpected ways. 'Affection' is one of those words in *The Winter's Tale*. A database called a concordance can be used to discover how many times a certain word appears in one or more plays of Shakespeare. According to the on-line OpenSourceShakespeare concordance, 'affection' appears seventy-eight times in Shakespeare's plays. Appearing infrequently in most plays, 'affection' shows up six times in *The Winter's Tale* and ten times in *Much Ado about Nothing*, a comedy about a woman falsely accused of sexual infidelity and hence an intertext for *The Winter's Tale*. In *The Winter's Tale*, 'jealousy' and 'jealousies' appear only once each (1.2.447, 4.1.18). Whereas Leontes is certainly motivated by jealousy, 'jealousy' does not carry the density of associations that 'affection' builds through its multiple appearances in the play. Below, you will have an opportunity to write about the meaning(s) of 'affection' at various moments during *The Winter's Tale*.

Finally, let's use the No Fear example to consider the interpretative consequences of even small editorial changes. First, whereas in the First Folio affection '[c]ommunicat'st *with* dreams', in No Fear's translation jealousy 'speaks *in* dreams'. Why might the SparkNotes editors have preferred 'speaks in dreams' to 'speaks with dreams', which would seem a more accurate translation of the original? How does the change of a single preposition change the meaning of the phrase? Second, by translating the First Folio's '[d]am' as 'mother', the SparkNotes editors eliminate the rich connotations of that early modern word. According to the *OED*, 'dam' is a variant of 'dame', meaning a female superior or ruler. As a queen, Hermione is certainly a dame, but that meaning of 'dam' had become obsolete by 1600. For the first audiences of *The Winter's Tale*, 'dam' would have signified primarily as the mother of an animal (dam *n*., 2a). Furthermore, the common expressions 'the devil and his dam' and 'the devil's dam', which appear several times in Shakespeare's plays, could be 'applied opprobriously to a woman' (dam *n*., 2b). 'Dam' also appears twice more in *The Winter's Tale*: Leontes insults Hermione as the 'dam' of a bastard, and Paulina praises Hermione as a 'gracious dam' (2.3.93, 3.2.195). Paulina's positive usage of 'dam' avoids its typically bestial or demonic connotations. In *Macbeth*, likewise, Macduff memorializes his murdered family as his 'pretty chickens, and their dam': a tender portrait of his wife as a nurturing mother (4.3.221). Shorn of such positive associations, Leontes's use of '[d]am' evokes bestial or demonic connotations appropriate to his suspicions of Hermione's sexual infidelity. The No Fear translation buries these connotations and the insight they offer into Leontes's state of mind. Going carefully through both the Pitcher and the No Fear version of Leontes's monologue, see if you can draw any conclusions about the effects of any other changes you notice.

In the end, this extremely challenging passage raises some general questions about the possibilities and limits of interpretation. How much do you need to understand to make sense of a given passage? Can we produce a significant, compelling reading of a passage even when some words, concepts or turns of thought elude us? Is it even possible to achieve complete comprehension of a passage? How would we know when we had done so? In an essay on 'The Poetics of Incomprehensibility', Stephen Orgel notes that

Leontes's 'Can thy Dam?' speech has 'defied any consensus' since eighteenth-century editors first tried to make sense of it (433). However, 'the Renaissance tolerated, and indeed courted, a much higher degree of ambiguity and opacity than we do; we tend to forget that the age often found in incomprehensibility a positive virtue' (Orgel, 'Poetics' 436). In other words, making sense of an opaque literary passage might be more important to us than it was to Shakespeare and his first readers and audience members. As Emma Smith writes of a similarly opaque speech in *Macbeth*, 'Shakespeare's speech is untranslatable, and its difficulties are intrinsic, not incidental. But the speech is also deeply enjoyable and memorable, not in spite, but because of, its complexity' (46-7). While you might not find Leontes's monologue particularly enjoyable, consider how its very complexity might make it memorable and effective at communicating feelings or ideas beyond the need for clarity.

Editorial additions: Stage directions

In addition to regularizing spelling, capitalization and punctuation, modern editors often add stage directions that 'allow us to visualize what happens when, who speaks to whom, which characters are present, and when they leave' (Erne 67). Let's look at an example of both original and editorial stage directions and consider their consequences for interpretation. A typical stage direction added by modern editors is the theatrical 'aside', which indicates words that a character speaks to themself, unheard by other characters. Square brackets around a stage direction – [*aside*] – signal that this stage direction is a later editorial addition that does not appear in a quarto or folio text. In the example below from Pitcher's edition of *The Winter's Tale*, Leontes and Camillo are discussing Hermione's success at persuading Polixenes to stay in Sicily. Pitcher adds an [*aside*] to indicate where Leontes's aside begins and a dash (–) to indicate where it ends.

> CAMILLO
> He would not stay at your petitions, made
> His business more material.

LEONTES
    Didst perceive it?
    [*aside*] They're here with me already, whispering, rounding,
    'Sicilia is a so-forth.' 'Tis far gone
    When I shall gust it last. – How came't, Camillo,
    That he did stay?
CAMILLO
    At the good queen's entreaty.
                                              (1.2.213-18)

We might first ask why Pitcher thought it likely that Leontes speaks in aside here. What about Leontes's language suggests that he could be speaking to himself? The absence of an 'aside' direction in the First Folio does not necessarily mean that an aside could not be present; Folio stage directions are sparse, usually specifying only entrances, exits and music. For the sake of argument, however, let's remove Pitcher's editorial 'aside' and assume that Leontes speaks the entire passage to Camillo. Why might it make sense for Leontes to share these thoughts with Camillo? What kind of response might he hope to get? My aim here is not to argue that one reading of the passage is preferable to another or that Pitcher was wrong to add this stage direction to his edition of the play. Rather, my aim is to demonstrate that an editor's decisions can make some readings available even as they occlude others. The more aware you are of editorial changes, the more material you will have to develop your own original and compelling interpretations.

Now let's consider the significance of stage directions that indicate actions or theatrical effects. When Antigonus arrives in Bohemia, we know that he sets down the infant Perdita because of an 'implied stage direction': words spoken by a character that specify a particular action. Antigonus says to Perdita, 'There lie, and there thy character' (3.3.46). Because of the action suggested by 'there lie', Pitcher adds the following stage direction: [*Lays the baby down in a mantle, with a box and letters.*] (3.3.45 SD). Pitcher specifies the mantle (cloak), box and letters because Antigonus mentions Perdita's 'character' (documents explaining her identity), and because when the Shepherd later finds Perdita, he mentions a cloak and a box of gold. Likewise, Antigonus's observation 'The storm begins' prompts Pitcher to add the stage direction [*Thunder*], a sound effect created in early modern theatres by rolling cannon balls down a channel (3.3.48). To signify stormy weather, thunder was much easier to produce in the early modern theatre than rain or wind.

This same scene also happens to contain the most notorious stage direction in all of Shakespeare. Although it's difficult to tell exactly what's happening from Antigonus's words – 'A savage clamour! / Well may I get aboard. This is the chase. / I am gone for ever!' (3.3.55-7) – a First Folio stage direction makes it clear that the actor playing Antigonus is to '*Exit, pursued by a bear*' (3.3.57 SD). Pitcher prints this stage direction without square brackets because it is original, not editorial. Much has been written about the strangeness of this moment, including debate over whether the 'bear' in question was a trained animal or an actor wearing a bear skin; contemporary beliefs about bears; the possible reference to the sport of bear-baiting, which took place near the Globe Theatre; whether audiences might have reacted to the bear with horror, pleasure or confusion; and the bear's symbolic significance as a manifestation of either Leontes's tyrannical fierceness or of Hermione's vengeance or 'mammalian female generativity' (Quilligan 521; Bristol 159-61; Cooper 1-2; Duckert; Egan, 3; Gurr 424; Hunt, 'Bearing'; Loomis; O'Connor 381-2; Paster 275; Ravelhofer 307, 314-15; Stevens 136).

Although few stage directions have repaid as much scrutiny as this one, when reading *The Winter's Tale*, pay attention to how many stage directions are in fact editorial additions rather than original to the First Folio. Try to identify any implied stage directions in the language of a character that might have prompted an editor to insert a bracketed stage direction. When reading bracketed stage directions, do you always agree with the editor's description of the action taking place? Is it possible to imagine different actions, movements or sounds than those the editor suggests?

Fallen language in *The Winter's Tale*

Whatever Leontes's 'Can thy Dam?' monologue might mean, it starkly brings to the fore that language in *The Winter's Tale* is not simply a medium of communication, but a form of expression that might communicate more or less than the speaker intends, or even confound communication altogether. Philosopher Stanley Cavell describes the chaos unleashed by Leontes's jealousy as 'the inability to say what exists; to say whether, so to speak, language applies to anything' (197). *The Winter's Tale* returns to this problem of language again and again. Shakespeare explores the 'unreliability and inadequacy of language' throughout his playwriting career, with the major tragedies written before *The Winter's Tale* 'pos[ing] the greatest challenge to any kind of linguistic security' (McDonald, *Art* 181). Several critics, however, have identified especially severe problems with language in *The Winter's Tale*. Marion O'Connor, for instance, argues that '[v]erbal signification is not to be trusted' in this play that 'deploys dialogue of disturbing opacity, obscurity, and indeterminacy' (383). Howard Felperin refers to a 'loss of verbal innocence' through a 'fall into a condition of multivocality or equivocation' ('Tongue-tied' 9). Adam McKeown posits that *The Winter's Tale* is unique among Shakespeare's plays in continuously contrasting rhetorical speeches, which attempt to persuade others, to 'speeches in which rhetorical intentions are either cast aside or avoided entirely, in which reasonable speech becomes inadequate', or in which characters 'demonstrate or even admit that they do not know how to speak their minds at all' (120). Focusing on gender difference, Matthew Kendrick argues that Leontes's sense of male superiority requires him to 'subjugate Hermione to the unquestioned authority of his words'; this patriarchal system begins to collapse when Hermione uses 'her rhetorical skill in a manner that subjects the men to her discursive power' (702-3).

The Winter's Tale marks problems of linguistic equivocation, incomprehension, opaqueness, misdirection and miscommunication as particularly acute around issues of sexuality. A compelling instance of this phenomenon appears in Hermione's response to Leontes's baseless accusations:

HERMIONE   Sir,
  You speak a language that I understand not.
  My life stands in the level of your dreams,
  Which I'll lay down.
LEONTES   Your actions are my dreams.
  You had a bastard by Polixenes,
  And I but dreamed it.

(3.2.77-82)

Hermione objects that Leontes's false accusations are the product of his 'dreams' or fantasies, a private or encrypted kind of language that she does not understand; he responds sarcastically that he must then have dreamed that Hermione gave birth to a bastard. Certain that Hermione's 'actions' have been illicit, Leontes uses the infant's existence to justify the truth of his accusations, without acknowledging that the infant's status as legitimate (his child) or 'bastard' (Polixenes's child) is precisely the issue in contention. In other words, Leontes behaves as if the word 'bastard' self-evidently describes the infant instead of being a contestable *interpretation* of the infant as product of Hermione's supposed sexual transgressions. Later, we will explore more of these charged moments from the first part of the play, where the intertwined problems of language and sexuality are most pronounced.

As we have already seen, failures of language in *The Winter's Tale* do not always concern sexuality. The first instance of linguistic failure in the play is when Archidamus stammers about the inadequate hospitality of his nation. Linguistic failure is sometimes easily visible on the page, as here: 'We cannot with such magnificence – in so rare – I know not what to say' (1.1.12-13). The dashes indicate that Archidamus, unable to complete a coherent thought, is in effect interrupting himself. He finally gives up with a flat admission of linguistic inadequacy: 'I know not what to say.' Expressing a similar idea in his first words of the play, Polixenes confesses that were he to properly thank Leontes for his hospitality, he would be expressing those thanks for nine months; yet even such exorbitant speech would fail to pay the 'debt' of gratitude he owes (1.1.5-6). Extending the financial metaphor, Polixenes explains – in what he mistakenly hopes will be the final word on his departure – that Leontes should take his single 'we thank you' as a 'cipher' (zero) 'standing in rich place' (1.2.6-8): like the number zero at the end of a large sum (e.g. the final zero in 10,000), it is nothing in itself, but highly valuable in its expansive operation. By saying 'we thank you' just once, Polixenes thanks Leontes thousands of times, instead of actually having to articulate the individual 'thank yous' that would detain him in Sicily another nine months, thus racking up an additional debt of gratitude that he would have to pay off with thousands more thanks, to infinity. All of this, to be sure, is courtly compliment. But it is also an astonishingly compact and powerful way to represent how language always seems to undo itself, both communicating and thwarting communication in the same breath. If one can never express enough thanks, can one ever really leave? It's precisely to the point that Polixenes's elaborate rhetoric fails to convince Leontes to allow his departure, and that when Leontes calls on Hermione to persuade Polixenes to stay, her success sets off his destructive suspicions of infidelity.

Like Polixenes's image of one phrase multiplying exponentially, Hermione's first words also suggest how words can escape a speaker's ability to contain or limit their meaning. During Leontes's dialogue with Polixenes, Hermione has remained silent, enacting a conventionally female virtue and sign of 'deference to her husband and king' (Schalkwyk, 'A Lady's "Verily"' 247). When Leontes prompts her to speak – 'Tongue-tied, our queen? Speak you' (1.2.27) – Hermione answers, 'I had thought, sir, to have held my peace until / You had drawn oaths from him not to stay' (1.2.28-9). No longer silent, Hermione unleashes a linguistic power that might be perceived as erotic. The tongue is an instrument of sexual pleasure as well as speech; Leontes explicitly imagines his wife and friend '[k]issing with inside lip' (1.2.284). Hermione's language broaches an interpretive problem: how do we know when words that do not explicitly name sexual actions or organs might have sexual connotations? How do we know when someone is being deliberately bawdy or when bawdy meanings are unintended? Where does sexual meaning come from? For instance, when Leontes commends Hermione for having persuaded Polixenes to stay, she attests to women's pleasure at being praised:

> cram's with praise, and make's
> As fat as tame things. One good deed, dying tongueless,
> Slaughters a thousand waiting upon that.
> Our praises are our wages. You may ride's
> With one soft kiss a thousand furlongs ere
> With spur we heat an acre.
>
> (1.2.91-6)

Do Hermione's animal metaphors have an erotic connotation? Why or why not? Would erotic language be compatible with the metaphors of death and finance she also uses? Why or why not? Does it matter whether or not Hermione is aware of the possible erotic connotations of her words? Such questions are important not only because they raise our self-consciousness about what interpretative assumptions or methods we bring to our reading, but also because they expose similar interpretive dilemmas within the play. In other words, when Hermione speaks of female pleasure in Polixenes's presence, Leontes might wonder if she is openly flirting with Polixenes, if she is inadvertently communicating her erotic desires or if he is reading sexual desire into language that is 'innocent' of sexual intentions.

Earlier in this same scene, Polixenes had overtly connected linguistic innocence with sexual innocence. Recounting his childhood days with Leontes, Polixenes tells a kind of fairy tale that casts the two boys as pure, speechless animals:

> We were like twinned lambs that did frisk i'th'sun
> And bleat the one at th'other: what we changed
> Was innocence for innocence; we knew not
> The doctrine of ill-doing, nor dreamed
> That any did. Had we pursued that life,
> And our weak spirits ne'er been higher reared
> With stronger blood, we should have answered heaven
> Boldly, 'not guilty', the imposition cleared
> Hereditary ours.
>
> (1.2.67-75)

Polixenes nostalgically represents boyhood as a sunny paradise in which perfectly matched friends share innocence and joy: a same-sex echo of the biblical garden of Eden before God expelled Adam and Eve for disobeying his commandment not to eat of the Tree of Knowledge. Had Polixenes and Leontes been able to remain in this state of childhood grace – a time before sexual knowledge, before the 'stronger blood' of sexual excitement could 'rear' or erect their 'spirits' (sexual desires, penises) – they would have been able to avoid the '[h]ereditary' guilt of original sin: the Christian belief that all humans inherited the sin of disobedience from Adam and Eve and thus required salvation through Christ. For Polixenes, innocence of sexual knowledge is linked to innocence of speech; human language is superfluous in this Edenic realm. The only words that need to be spoken are addressed to God: the plea of 'not guilty' that would clear the boys of original sin.

Although fantasies of childhood innocence might be relatively benign, this one taps into male suspicion of female sexuality, with its corollary suspicion about female speech. From Polixenes' parable, Hermione draws the implied conclusion: that since Polixenes and Leontes were unable to remain in their same-sex paradise, they, like Adam and Eve, must have 'tripped' or fallen into sin at some point. Affirming that reasoning, Polixenes retorts that their boyhood innocence was cut short by 'temptations' in the form of Hermione and Polixenes's (nameless) wife. Although Polixenes is complimenting Hermione for her tempting beauty, she teasingly warns him not to draw the ultimate conclusion from his reasoning. For if the women's beauty incited Polixenes and Leontes to sin, then Hermione and Polixenes's wife would be 'devils', who in Christian belief used deceptive language to tempt humans into damnable deeds (1.2.82). Although Polixenes and Hermione are engaging in witty courtly banter and not serious theological debate, their conversation touches on troubling beliefs about the erotic power of female speech that have already begun to torment Leontes (van Elk 436). Precisely at this juncture, Leontes praises Hermione for having persuaded Polixenes to stay; moments later, Leontes expresses his suspicions of her infidelity. Via analogy with Polixenes's Edenic fantasy, we might refer to this equivocal, deceptive, sexualized speech as 'fallen'.

Once he acknowledges the possibility of sexual betrayal, Leontes's own language keeps sliding into sexual innuendo, as if he can no longer prevent dark libidinous energies from breaking through the surface of civilized thought and speech. Instructing Mamillius to keep his face clean or 'neat' in accordance with rules of social refinement, Leontes recalls that a 'neat' is a calf, whose horns remind him of the cuckold's horns (1.2.123). Although Leontes creates a more positive association with horned beasts by affectionately calling Mamillius a 'wanton' (wild) calf, 'wanton' also commonly signified sexual promiscuity. In a speech remarkably dense with sexual imagery, Leontes laments his fate as a cuckold:

> There have been,
> Or I am much deceived, cuckolds ere now,
> And many a man there is even at this present,
> Now, while I speak this, holds his wife by th'arm,
> That little thinks she has been sluiced in's absence,

> And his pond fished by his next neighbour, by
> Sir Smile, his neighbour. Nay, there's comfort in't,
> Whiles other men have gates, and those gates opened,
> As mine, against their will.
>
> (1.2.189-97)

Although Leontes 'comfort[s]' himself with the knowledge that 'many' men are cuckolds, that very commonness vexes him, as his sovereignty should make him absolutely singular (Cormack 490). Leontes identifies with the humiliation of a common villager who doesn't realize that his neighbour is having sex with his wife. Take a closer look at the language Leontes uses to describe this homely scene of domestic treachery. First, remember that we can sometimes see language falling apart or slipping into incoherence on the page, as we noticed with Archidamus's stumbling language in 1.1. Note how many times in this short passage Leontes uses qualifying phrases and repeated words. What are the effects of these patterns on the flow of his speech? How does Leontes use metaphors of water and gates to convey the idea of sexual infidelity? What roles do these metaphors assign to the wife, the husband and the neighbour in this domestic drama? Why does he call the neighbour 'Sir Smile'?

Finally, Leontes's certainty that he has been 'infected' by knowledge of sexual betrayal brings us full circle from Polixenes's narrative of an Edenic boyhood prior to language and sex (2.1.41-2). When Leontes accuses Hermione of adultery, he insists that the monstrousness of her crime has in effect corrupted language itself. He instructs his (male) courtiers:

> Look on her, mark her well. Be but about
> To say she is a goodly lady, and
> The justice of your hearts will thereto add
> 'Tis pity she's not honest, honourable.
> Praise her but for this her without-door form –
> Which on my faith deserves high speech – and straight
> The shrug, the hum or ha, these petty brands
> That calumny doth use – O, I am out!
> That mercy does, for calumny will sear
> Virtue itself – these shrugs, these hums and ha's,
> When you have said she's goodly, come between
> Ere you can say she's honest.
>
> (2.1.65-76)

As with Leontes's speech about cuckoldry above, fallen language manifests on the page as parenthetical interruptions, disruptive punctuation, repeated words and broken sentences. Here, however, Leontes is talking explicitly about the problem of finding a language adequate for describing the paradox that is Hermione. According to Leontes, why would observers insert 'shrugs' (verbal pauses or reservations) such as 'hum' or 'ha' into their praise of Hermione's beauty? Are such interjections signs that the speaker intends to speak 'calumny' (slander) or to speak with 'mercy' of Hermione? Why might Leontes use legal terms such as 'mercy' and 'justice' to convey the dilemma of describing Hermione's beauty (2.1.78)?

Ultimately, Leontes suggests that Hermione's paradoxical status as a dishonourable queen threatens to throw civilized order itself into chaos. Unable anymore to call Hermione a 'queen', he can only identify her as an object:

> O thou thing,
> Which I'll not call a creature of thy place,
> Lest barbarism, making me the precedent,
> Should a like language use to all degrees,
> And mannerly distinguishment leave out
> Betwixt the prince and beggar.
>
> (2.1.82-7)

As we did with Leontes's 'Can thy Dam?' monologue, let's consider a (possible) paraphrase of this passage before analysing its nuances, connotations and associations:

> I cannot properly name what you are. If I were to continue to address you as queen (which, having lost your honor, you no longer truly are), I would set a precedent for the abuse of language. Following my bad example, uncivilized peoples might use the same words to address people of different social ranks, thus failing properly to distinguish the highborn from the lowborn.

Returning to the passage, let's focus on some important words omitted from my paraphrase. First, in dehumanizing Hermione, 'thing' might also degrade her sexually, as slang for the vagina (Pitcher 2.1.82n.).

Although 'creature' might simply mean 'human being', it might also mean a 'reprehensible or despicable person' or an animal (*OED* creature *n.*, 2c, 3a). Once again, Leontes's purportedly civilized language unleashes hostile sexual and animalistic meanings. The words 'barbarism', 'degrees' and 'mannerly' are significantly linked. 'Barbarism' is an explicitly linguistic term, referring to 'rudeness or unpolished condition of language'; by extension it could mean 'uncivilized ignorance and rudeness' (*OED* barbarism *n.*, 1a, 2a). As the antithesis of civilization, 'barbarism' often had explicitly ethnic or racial connotations in Shakespeare's England, designating the supposedly 'primitive, socially inferior or dangerous' condition of Africans (Ian Smith 5). 'Mannerly' likewise refers to norms of civilization via its derivation from 'manners': 'well-mannered, polite' (*OED* mannerly *adj.*, 3). Finally, 'degrees' reminds us that social ranks are not only differential – beggars are not princes – but hierarchical: beggars are many degrees or steps beneath princes on the social scale. What conclusions can you draw from Leontes's fear that his treatment of Hermione will set a 'precedent' for barbaric speech? According to Leontes, what is the civilized response to Hermione's adultery? How does Leontes's concern with fallen language here relate to the other instances of fallen language we have considered in the first part of *The Winter's Tale*?

Writing matters

In the following pages, you will find options for using writing to develop the research and interpretative skills introduced in this chapter, including paraphrasing, using a concordance and evaluating the consequences of editorial changes to the First Folio text. You will also have an opportunity to develop your ideas on the topic of fallen language in *The Winter's Tale*.

Working with paraphrase

In analysing Leontes's 'Can thy Dam?' speech, we saw that while paraphrase can clarify the basic meaning of a difficult passage, it can also sacrifice the ambiguity, nuance, mystery and even beauty of Shakespeare's language. For this writing exercise, (1) write a one-paragraph paraphrase of *one* of the following passages: 1.2.34-44 (Hermione), 1.2.108-19 (Leontes) or 1.2.387-95 (Polixenes); (2) in one or two paragraphs, explain in detail what you did in the paraphrase to convert the passage into your own words (i.e. explicating metaphors, substituting modern words for early modern words, summarizing complex ideas, simplifying syntax etc.); (3) in a final paragraph, analyse what is lost from the passage in the paraphrase. You might consider the following questions in your analysis. Does your paraphrase eliminate any of the play's 'keywords': significant words that can be traced (using a concordance) throughout the play? If your paraphrase eliminates any homonyms (e.g. 'mettle','metal') or words with double meanings (e.g. 'satisfy' meaning both 'to please' and 'to have sex with'), what is the effect of those eliminations? Rereading the passage in light of your paraphrase, which words, images or figures of speech give the former its energy, power or complexity? What does the particular language used by the speaker in the passage reveal about the speaker's values, beliefs or motives? What elements of the passage seem difficult or impossible to paraphrase, and why?

Working with visual imagery

This exercise builds on the paraphrase exercise by exploring the limits and possibilities of language in a different way: by translation to the medium of the visual. (1) Choose *one* of the following passages that contain dense and complex images: 1.1.22-31, 1.2.197-205, 2.1.39-45, 3.2.206-11 or 4.4.350-7; (2) create a visual image (in whatever medium works best for you) of what is being described in the passage; (3) explain how you translated the language of the passage into a visual image, and with what results. For instance, does your visual image manage to convey something more effectively or powerfully than the language of the passage? If so, you might explain how visual representation might offer resources for comprehension (e.g. shape, colour, scale, dimension, position) that surpass those of linguistic representation. At the same time, as with the paraphrase exercise, you might ask yourself if your visual rendition of the passage omits, simplifies or stabilizes ambiguities that enhance the complexity and impact of Shakespeare's language.

Working with a concordance

Choose *one* of the following options:

   1 Examine the six instances of the keyword 'affection' in *The Winter's Tale*: 1.1.24, 1.2.138, 4.4.384, 4.4.485-6, 5.1.219 and 5.2.36. Choose any *three* of these instances and devote a paragraph each to explicating the contextual meaning and significance of 'affection' in that passage. In a final paragraph, draw some conclusions about how 'affection' connects these passages, even if it does not mean exactly the same thing in each passage.
   2 Choose any word from *The Winter's Tale* that you suspect might carry a complex set of meanings or associations. Here are some suggestions, arbitrarily chosen: 'whispering', 'white'/'whiteness', 'blood', 'infected', 'ignorant', 'issue'. Look up your word in a concordance and read the passages in which the word appears. Choose any *three* of these instances and devote a paragraph each to explicating the contextual meaning and significance of your word in that passage. In a final paragraph, draw some conclusions about how your word connects these passages, even if it does not mean exactly the same thing in each passage.

Working with editorial stage directions

In this chapter we explored how editors of Shakespeare often add stage directions that do not appear in the earliest published texts of the plays in order to clarify what a character is doing or to whom a character is speaking. Consider the following passage from Pitcher's edition of *The Winter's Tale*:

> LEONTES   So have we thought it good
> From our free person she should be confined,
> Lest that the treachery of the two fled hence
> Be left her to perform. Come, follow us,
> We are to speak in public; for this business
> Will raise us all.

ANTIGONUS
  [*aside*] To laughter, as I take it,
  If the good truth were known.

(2.1.193-9)

Pitcher adds an [*aside*] to indicate his belief that Antigonus speaks these words to himself or possibly to the audience – in any case, not to Leontes. What if we omit Pitcher's stage direction? In a paragraph or two, use evidence from the play to argue that it makes excellent sense for Antigonus to speak these words directly to Leontes. You might consider addressing the following issues. Why might a modern editor believe that Antigonus is speaking in aside? What counter-arguments could you offer to support the view that Antigonus is speaking to Leontes? Are these words consistent with the way Antigonus addresses Leontes elsewhere in the play? Might Antigonus speak the line so that not only Leontes, but also the other characters present, can hear it? If so, why might Antigonus want the other lords to hear what he says? If Antigonus's comment is meant for Leontes to hear, why doesn't Leontes respond to it (Antigonus's words close the scene)? Could you imagine a performance in which Leontes reacts in a non-verbal way to Antigonus's comment?

Analysing fallen language

Earlier, I suggested that failed communication accounts in part for the tragic escalation of Leontes's jealousy. This exercise gives you the chance to explore that hypothesis through an analysis of Leontes's speech to Camillo in 1.2.265-76, either in the First Folio version (reproduced below), or in a modern edition of *The Winter's Tale*. If you decide to work with the Folio passage, you should address what its punctuation might signal about the character's state of mind or how the actor might have delivered these lines. If you believe that any of the capitalized words are particularly significant, you can also explain why. Whichever version of the passage you choose, perform a close reading that makes an argument about how Leontes's jealousy impacts his language. You might wish to address the following issues in your analysis. How might Leontes's emotional agitation affect the way he speaks? How in control of his language does he seem to be? What does he want from Camillo here? What is Leontes saying about seeing, hearing and thinking in this passage? What do seeing, hearing and thinking have to do with Hermione's supposed adultery? What kind of language does Leontes use to describe Hermione and her actions in this passage? How would you describe the tone (or emotional colouring) of this passage?

From the First Folio:

Ha'not you seene *Camillo*?
(But that's past doubt: you have, or your eye-glasse
Is thicker then a Cuckolds Horne) or heard?
(For to a Vision so apparant, Rumor
Cannot be mute) or thought? (for Cogitation,
Resides not in that man, that do's not thinke)
My Wife is slipperie? If thou wilt confesse,
Or else be impudently negative,
To have nor Eyes, nor Eares, nor Thought, then say
My Wife's a Holy-Horse,[1] deserves a Name
As ranke as any Flax-Wench, that puts to
Before her troth-plight: say't, and justify't.

---

[1]Pitcher proposes that this is a clear misprint for 'Hobby-Horse', a term used in early modern England for promiscuous women.

2

Language: Style and form

In Chapter One we began a detailed examination of the language of *The Winter's Tale* by analysing how individual words functioned to convey characters' values, motives and emotions. We also addressed how original typographical details such as capitalization, punctuation and italics might have conveyed meaning. Finally, we looked at the problem of fallen language in the first part of the play, manifested especially in the infection of courtly speech with sexual meanings. In this chapter, we move from small units of meaning such as the individual word and the punctuation mark to larger units of meaning: the styles and forms of language – prose, verse, soliloquy, oration, reporting and rhetorical figures – that shape character, action and structure in *The Winter's Tale*.

We will start with the most fundamental linguistic distinction in Shakespearean drama: that between writing in verse and writing in prose. We will consider how, why and when characters speak in verse or prose, and what either style might (or might not) convey about character, mood, genre or situation. Approaching Shakespeare's unrhymed verse as a flexible medium of expression, we will become familiar with tools for analysing the metre (patterns of stressed or unstressed syllables), rhythm and sound of dramatic verse. Turning to the forms of dramatic speech, we will consider why Leontes has so many soliloquies early in the play and examine what their rhetoric might reveal about his desires, values or beliefs. We will then broaden our scope from the private soliloquy to Hermione's use of rhetorical modes of address in her public formal oration. The chapter concludes with a discussion of the dramatic functions of reporting in *The Winter's Tale*.

Prose, verse and rhyme

Let's begin by considering the different implications and effects of prose and verse in *The Winter's Tale*. Almost every statement that we might make about this topic should come with the caveat that Shakespeare did not follow any strict rules when it came to writing verse or prose. Whenever critics generalize about some tendency in Shakespeare's writing – be it generic structures, rhetorical habits, character psychology, stylistic distinctions between the earlier and later plays etc. – we should both consider the validity of that position and acknowledge the significance of any exceptions.

You have probably heard the claim that in Shakespeare's plays elite characters speak verse and commoners speak prose. It's true that Shakespeare's elite characters *usually* speak verse because early modern rhetoricians generally considered poetry more elevated and formal than prose. Douglas Bruster explains that when 'contrasted with verse (as it so often was), prose was typically held to feature opposite traits and aspects, or, at the very least, less positive attributes' than those of poetry (101). Shakespeare's contemporaries typically regarded prose as 'less formal, less authoritative, less beautiful', than verse, as well as more 'tedious' and verbose (Bruster 101). According to Bruster, Shakespeare usually uses verse for characters who of are 'high rank', 'educated' and speak 'proper English'; in 'formal', 'serious' and 'ceremonial' situations (particularly in tragedy); and to express 'sentiment' or 'decorum' (105). In contrast, Shakespeare usually uses prose for characters who are of 'middle and low rank', 'uneducated' and speak 'non-standard English'; in 'informal', 'playful' and 'commercial' situations (particularly in comedy); and to express 'satire', 'criticism' or 'obscenity' (105). We can observe these tendencies in *The Winter's Tale*. Leontes, Hermione, Paulina and Florizel speak only in verse. The formal, ceremonial and generically tragic trial of Hermione is conducted entirely in verse, with the important exception of written documents that are read aloud. As Bruster's schema would suggest, Autolycus's playful, satirical and commercial interactions with the Bohemian shepherds take place in prose.

Although it is *generally* true that in *The Winter's Tale* Shakespeare uses verse for educated and elite characters and prose for uneducated and low-status characters, this social mapping of style should not be taken as a 'fixed principle', since significant exceptions can be found (Barish, 'Mixed' 57). Aristocratic characters in particular demonstrate the flexibility to 'downshift' into prose when circumstances call for it. For instance, the play's two major scenes of courtly reporting (1.1. and 5.2) are in prose. As we saw in Chapter One, the play opens with Camillo and Archidamus giving an account of the two kings' friendship and Mamillius's future promise. In 5.2, the discovery of Perdita's identity takes place offstage but is reported at length by several court officers. Shakespeare might have felt that prose, with its facility for prolixity, was the best vehicle for the exposition of these histories and events. Polixenes and Camillo converse entirely in prose throughout 4.2, even echoing the topics discussed by Archidamus and Camillo in 1.1: the relationship between the two kings and the disposition of a kingdom's heir. In an accommodation typically made by Shakespeare's aristocrats when communicating with prose-speaking social inferiors, Polixenes speaks prose with the Shepherd and a rustic servant during the sheep-shearing festival (4.4).

Although prose is often assigned to poor or uneducated characters, it would be a mistake to regard prose in Shakespeare as plain or artless speech. Passages of prose can be 'highly structured': they 'seem to utilise visible and audible rhetorical or syntactical patterns as a way of compensating for the absence of metrical structure' (Barish, 'Mixed' 62). We might expect artful patterns in the prose of educated characters. For example, a Gentleman says of the court's reaction to the discovery of Perdita's identity that '[t]here was speech in their dumbness, language in their very gesture. They looked as they had heard of a world ransomed, or one destroyed' (5.2.13-15). The parallelism of these lines is striking: 'speech in their dumbness' is matched by 'language in their... gesture'; a 'world ransomed' is antithetically answered by 'one destroyed'.

It is not only the elite, however, who speak complex prose. For instance, upon discovering the infant Perdita, the old Shepherd speaks the following monologue:

> What have we here? Mercy on's, a bairn [child]! A very pretty bairn. A boy or a child [girl], I wonder? A pretty one, a very pretty one – sure some scape; though I am not bookish, yet I can read waiting-gentlewoman in the scape. This has been some stair-work, some trunk-work, some behind-door-work.
>
> (3.3.68-73)

Rhetorical patterning is present in the repetitions of 'bairn' and 'pretty' and in the alliteration that attends the Shepherd's speculation about the circumstances of the infant's conception: *sure some scape*. Since uneducated characters usually speak prose, it's ironic that the Shepherd uses a rather sophisticated metaphor when commenting that despite not being 'bookish' – used to reading – he can nonetheless 'read' the cause of the infant's abandonment in a servant's need to conceal her sexual indiscretion. Imagining where the conception took place, the Shepherd uses a series of compound nouns, each of which links a domestic setting with 'work' as a euphemism for 'fornication': 'some stair-work, some trunk-work, some back-door-work'. In fact, that sequence of grammatically parallel phrases – some *x*, some *y*, some *z* – is an example of the classical rhetorical figure called isocolon. What are the effects of the Shepherd's artful speech? Do his rhetorical abilities suggest that despite his rustic existence he has some knowledge of sophisticated social mores and conventions? Does his rhetoric reassure us that Perdita's adoptive father will give her a moderately refined, if humble, upbringing? Whatever conclusions we might draw from this particular case, it leads to an important insight: more informative than simply noting which characters speak verse or prose is understanding *how* and *why* characters speak the way they do, when they do and to whom.

In addition to focusing on the speech patterns of individual characters, we can take a wider view of Shakespeare's shifts between prose and verse within a scene or between scenes. Jonas Barish observes that there are many cases in which 'a new scene coincides with a shift from prose to verse or its opposite, as new characters, new topics of discourse, a new social milieu, or a new emotional climate, come into view' ('Mixed' 55). Similarly, Russ McDonald posits that when Shakespeare introduces prose, it 'signals an alteration of mood, a relaxation of tension, a tonal variation that influences the audience whether or not they are conscious of the shift' (116). An excellent illustration of how alteration of speech styles can mark changes in milieu or mood appears in the sequence of scenes that form the crucial transition from the first part to the second part of *The Winter's Tale*.

A shift from verse to prose marks the generic and tonal shift from tragedy to comedy at the centre of the play. Antigonus's abandonment of Perdita in Bohemia (3.3), a serious and mournful scene, is composed in verse. Antigonus's last words, delivered as he flees from a bear – 'I am gone for ever!' – aptly form an incomplete verse line (a line of fewer than ten syllables) to stress that his life has been cut short (3.3.57). Immediately thereafter, the Shepherd enters talking to himself in prose: the expected medium for an uneducated labourer and his son, the Clown, a foolish rustic. The Clown's use of incongruously homely images when reporting the horrible deaths he has witnessed helps to distance the seriousness of these events. For instance, he describes the sinking ship as 'swallowed with yeast and froth, as you'd thrust a cork into a hogshead': a cask filled with ale (3.3.91-2). Even as he marks these deaths as 'heavy matters', the Shepherd uses artfully balanced prose to announce the generic transition from tragedy to comedy: 'Thou met'st with things dying, I with things newborn' (3.3.109-11).

Another significant tonal shift occurs when Shakespeare introduces Time, the only character in the play to speak in rhymed couplets: paired rhyming lines in a pattern of *aa* ('terror'/'error'), *bb* ('Time'/'crime'), *cc* ('slide'/'untried') and so on (4.1.1-6). The artificiality of rhymed couplets transports us from the everyday world of the rustics into a more formal, elevated realm. The rhymed words that connect the two lines of each couplet also potentially convey meaning through their phonic similarities. Consider how the juxtaposition of 'terror'/'error', 'power'/'hour', or 'stale'/'tale' might encapsulate Time's role in the play (1-2, 7-8, 13-14). Whereas the Shepherd concludes the previous scene with informal prose – '''Tis a lucky, day, boy, and we'll do good deeds on't' (3.3.135-6) – Time begins his speech with an emphatic 'I' and balanced, antithetical phrasing: 'I, that please some, try all; both joy and terror / Of good and bad, that makes and unfolds error' (4.1.1-2). Time's antitheses, moreover, remove him from 'any specific cultural frame of reference' such as a particular locale or era (Zender 107): he can 'in one self-born hour' both 'plant' and 'o'erwhelm custom'; he has existed unchanged since 'ancient'st order was' to 'what is now' (8-11). The thorny syntax and abstractions of Time's language require a different kind of attention than the plainer, colloquial, language of the Shepherd and his son.

A final sequence of stylistic contrasts completes the transition between the Sicilian and Bohemian parts of the play. Although Polixenes and Camillo are high-ranking characters who would normally speak verse, their prose conversation in 4.2 conveys their comfortable familiarity as well as signals the possibility that

Bohemia will be a more relaxed milieu than Sicily. Whereas Leontes never speaks in prose, Polixenes is evidently comfortable in a more casual linguistic register. The unremarkably pragmatic language that concludes Polixenes's plotting – 'My best Camillo! We must disguise ourselves' (4.2.54) – gives way in the next scene to a vibrant song, in rhyme, performed by a new character, Autolycus. All rhyme is not the same. Whereas Time speaks in rhymed couplets (*aa*, *bb*, etc.), Autolycus sings using an alternating rhyme scheme typical of musical lyrics (*abab*, *cdcd*, etc.). Songs in Shakespeare always rhyme, and usually stick to a regular metrical pattern in order to accommodate the music that would be repeated for each verse. Autolycus's song takes unusual liberties with meter. For contrast's sake, consider the highly regular meter of another song about the spring, from *Love's Labor's Lost*:

> When daisies pied and violets blue
> And lady-smocks all silver-white
> And cuckoo-buds of yellow hue
> Do paint the meadows with delight
>
> (5.2.880-3)

Each of these lines is written in perfect iambic tetrameter (eight-syllable lines comprising an unstressed syllable followed by a stressed syllable). Now compare the rhythms of Autolycus's song. Where does the song appear to conform to or depart from strict tetrameter?

> When daffodils begin to peer,
> With heigh, the doxy over the dale,
> Why then comes in the sweet o'the year,
> For the red blood reigns in the winter's pale.
>
> The white sheet bleaching on the hedge,
> With heigh, the sweet birds, O how they sing!
> Doth set my pugging tooth an edge,
> For a quart of ale is a dish for a king.
>
> (4.3.1-8)

Compared to 'When Daisies Pied', the lines in Autolycus's song show variation in both metre and length: the number of syllables in each line could be mapped as 8, 9, 9, 10 (stanza one), and 8, 9, 8, 11 (stanza two). The third stanza continues this variance; it contains lines of 8, 9, 9 and 8 syllables. What significance might you attribute to the irregularity of Autolycus's song?

Although he sings in verse, Autolycus, as a poor, low-status, character, speaks in prose while he is alone on stage and later in conversation with the Clown, whom he robs using a witty con act (4.3). Exiting the scene as he had entered it, Autolycus sings a single verse in the usual *abab* rhyme pattern: 'Jog on, jog on, the footpath way, / And merrily hent the stile-a' (4.3.122-3). In contrast to Autolycus's bouncing, jittery, rhythms, the sheep-shearing scene opens with Florizel speaking the smooth, elegant verse appropriate for a young aristocratic lover: 'These your unusual weeds to each part of you / Does give a life; no shepherdess, but Flora / Peering in April's front' (4.4.1-3). Although both Autolycus and Florizel open their respective scenes with imagery of spring flowers, Autolycus's rhymed song brashly celebrates the 'red blood' of sexual stimulation and consummation (4.3.4), whereas Florizel's unrhymed verse temperately praises Perdita's regal costume for its enlivening effects.

Finally, a significant stylistic feature of the festival scene are the songs that Autolycus sings to advertise his goods and the ballads that he sells to the Clown. Autolycus enters the sheep-shearing festival singing a typical peddler's song, written in tetrameter couplets, that enumerates his wares: 'Lawn as white as driven snow, / Cypress black as e'er was crow' (4.4.220-1). Autolycus also peddles ballads, song lyrics that were printed on a single sheet of paper. Instead of supplying the music, the ballad sheet would identify a familiar tune to which its lyrics could be sung. To advertise their ballads to passers-by, peddlers typically sang them in the streets. Mass-produced and costing only a penny, ballads were a significant form of inexpensive popular culture in the early modern period. Autolycus's ballads are typically sensationalistic: he offers a serious ballad about a usurer's wife who gives birth to 'twenty money-bags'; a 'pitiful' ballad of a hard-hearted maid transformed into a singing fish; and a 'merry' ballad to be sung to the tune of 'Two Maids Wooing a Man' (263, 281, 289-90). Mopsa and Dorcas, who already know the tune, join Autolycus in singing the ballad. Whereas no songs appear in the tragic first three acts of *The Winter's Tale*, Shakespeare fills Bohemia with music, from Autolycus's initial song about the seasons (4.3.1-12); to the music accompanying dances of shepherds, shepherdesses and rustics dressed as satyrs (4.4.167, 347 SD); to peddler's songs and ballads. Given the proliferation of popular music in Bohemia, consider the significance of the next and final appearance of music in *The Winter's Tale*: Paulina's command to animate Hermione's statue: 'Music, awake her; strike!' (5.3.98). What kind of music might be appropriate for this moment?

Analysing Shakespeare's blank verse

The next few sections of this chapter will address the components that contribute to the artistry of Shakespeare's verse in *The Winter's Tale*. Most of the play is written in blank verse, a term from Shakespeare's own time that describes unrhymed (hence 'blank') poetry composed in iambic pentameter lines. Meter is the essence of poetry, and the effective use of meter involves the establishment and variation of rhythmic patterns. Russ McDonald writes of the 'sense of expectation that poetic form stimulates in the perceiver. In most English poetry, a listener hears the reiterated rhythm, presumes and desires that it will continue, and notices when it changes or fails' (79). Below, we will attend to the 'reiterated rhythm' of Shakespeare's blank verse by analysing the length of lines and the alternation of stressed and unstressed syllables within lines. Then we'll consider how Shakespeare thwarts our 'sense of expectation' by altering the length, flow or stresses of the verse line.

It's helpful to begin by familiarizing yourself with some basic terms for analysing poetic meter and rhythm. Understanding these terms will help you to recognize and describe how Shakespeare creates a regular poetic line and also how and why he might disrupt the regularity of a line. The first set of terms below concern poetic meter; the next set of terms is used to identify pauses or continuities in a poetic line; the final three terms describe poetic lines that are longer or shorter than the established norm. Next we'll look at some terms for identifying sound effects in poetry. Finally, we'll use these terms to analyse some passages from *The Winter's Tale*. The primary purpose of this analysis will be to demonstrate how attention to the rhythms and sounds of blank verse can facilitate original and compelling interpretations.

Terms for meter

iamb: a poetic foot composed of an unstressed syllable followed by a **stressed** syllable.
Ex.: comp**elled**.

iambic pentameter: a verse line comprised of five iambic feet, or ten syllables. Use the symbol | to separate poetic feet.
Ex.: What **stud** | ied **tor** | ments, **ty** | rant, **hast** | for **me** (3.2.172).
     1   2   3   4   5   6   7   8   9 10 =
                                           ten syllables
    foot | foot | foot | foot | foot =
                                          five feet = pentameter

trochee: a poetic foot composed of a **stressed** syllable followed by an unstressed syllable.
Ex: **hope**ful.

spondee: a poetic foot composed of a **stressed** syllable followed by a **stressed** syllable.
Ex.: **gross hag!** (2.3.106).

pyrrhic: a poetic foot composed of an unstressed syllable followed by an unstressed syllable.
Ex.: O **cut** | my **lace,** | lest my | **heart, crack** | ing it (3.2.170).
     iamb | iamb | pyrrhic | spondee | pyrrhic

Terms for pausing or continuing a verse line

end-stopped: a verse line that ends with punctuation, thus requiring a pause or stop at the line break.
Ex.: The keeper of the prison, call to him.
    Let him have knowledge who I am. (2.2.1-2).
Because of the period end-stops, each of Paulina's two sentences corresponds exactly to the length of a single verse line.

enjambment: the running over of one verse line into the next in the absence of an end stop.
Ex.: Though I am satisfied, and need no more
    Than what I know.... (2.1.189-90)

caesura: a break within the verse line, often in the middle ('medial caesura'), but sometimes near the beginning ('initial') or end ('terminal'). Use the symbol ‖ to notate a caesura.
Ex: You are abused, ‖ and by some putter-on
 That will be damned for't. ‖ Would I knew the villain,
 I would land-damn him. ‖ Be she honour-flawed,... (2.1.141-3)
Each of these lines contains a medial caesura. The first line is enjambed; the second and third are end-stopped.

Terms for the length of a line

short line: a verse line that contains fewer syllables than those prescribed by the meter.
Ex.: Do not you fear. Upon mine honour, I
 Will stand betwixt you and danger.(2.2.63-4)
Whereas the first line is in regular iambic pentameter (ten syllables), the second line contains only eight syllables.

feminine ending: an extra unstressed syllable at the end of a verse line.
Ex.: Be cer | tain **what** | you **do,** | **sir,** lest | your **jus** | tice... (2.1.127). The eleventh syllable ('-tice') of this long line [see below] is unstressed.

long (extrametrical) line: a verse line that contains more syllables than those prescribed by the meter.
Ex.: I am as ignorant in that as you
 In so entitling me, and no less honest (2.3.68-9).
Whereas the first line is in regular iambic pentameter (ten syllables), the second line contains eleven syllables (and a feminine ending).

Terms for sound

alliteration: The repetition of initial consonant sounds in verse.
Ex.: He straight *d*eclined, *d*rooped, took it *d*eeply (2.3.13).

LANGUAGE: STYLE AND FORM

<u>assonance</u>: The repetition of vowel sounds in verse.
Ex.: Th<u>e</u> queen, th<u>e</u> qu<u>ee</u>n,
Th<u>e</u> sw<u>ee</u>test, d<u>ea</u>rest, cr<u>ea</u>ture's d<u>ea</u>d, and v<u>e</u>ng<u>ea</u>nce for't
N<u>o</u>t dr<u>o</u>pped d<u>o</u>wn y<u>et</u>' (3.2.197-9).
These lines contain four repeated vowel sounds: (1) the <u>e</u> in 'the'; (2) the <u>ee</u> in 'queen'; (3) the <u>ea</u> in 'dead'; (4) the <u>o</u> in 'not'.

<u>consonance</u>: The repetition of consonant sounds in verse.
Ex.: I*n*noce*n*ce for i*n*noce*n*ce; we *k*new *n*ot (1.2.69).

<u>internal rhyme</u>: The rhyming of words within a verse line or lines (not exclusively at the end of lines).
Ex.: But let him say *so* then, and let him *go* (1.2.35).

<u>onomatopoeia</u>: The naming of a thing through a word that imitates the sound of that thing.
Ex.: whose issue / Will *hiss* me to my grave (1.2.188).

Now let's analyse how all these poetic traits – meter, flow, length and sound – come together to give shape and meaning to a short passage from *The Winter's Tale*. In this passage, Hermione speaks to Leontes about Polixenes' desire to return to Bohemia.

To tell he longs to see his son were strong;
But let him say so then, and let him go;
But let him swear so and he shall not stay,
We'll thwack him hence with distaffs.

(1.2.34-7)

The remarkable uniformity of Hermione's language establishes a pattern that is disrupted by the irregular final line. In the first three lines, Hermione invites Polixenes to articulate ('tell', 'say', 'swear') his desire to leave Sicily. Suddenly moving from speech to action, the final line blossoms into a comical image of Hermione and her ladies using distaffs (rods used by women to spin flax) to beat Polixenes out of court. Every word in the speech is monosyllabic except the last, a shift in pattern that places significant emphasis on 'distaffs' and the visual image it evokes. The ladies' vigorous actions are underscored by the only unusual word in the speech, 'thwack', which via onomatopoeia conveys the sound of a blow. A concordance confirms the rarity of 'thwack', which appears in only two of Shakespeare's plays, once in *The Winter's Tale* and three times (in close proximity) in *Coriolanus*. Through repeated words and balanced phrases – 'but let him say so', 'let him go', 'but let him swear so' – punctuated by end-stopped lines and supported by the internal rhyme of 'so' and 'go', Hermione's argument builds to a seemingly inevitable conclusion. The consistency of alliteration in this speech contributes to its tight argument: every word begins with a *t*, *h*, *l*, or *s* except for a few beginning with *w* ('were', 'we'll', 'with'), *b* ('but'), *g* ('go'), *a* ('and'), *n* ('not'), and *d* ('distaffs'). Moreover, each line is in perfect iambic pentameter except the last, which ends abruptly after seven syllables in accordance with the indecorous and unexpected image of ladies expelling a visiting monarch with domestic implements. The empty space after the short line also allows an opportunity for the actor playing Hermione to pause for audience laughter, or to turn fully towards Polixenes, to whom she now begins to speak (Rokison 297).

Let's consider another speech that contains greater metrical variation than the example above. Polixenes here gives an account of his bond with his young son:

He's all my exercise, my mirth, my matter;
Now my sworn friend, and then mine enemy;
My parasite, my soldier, statesman, all.
He makes a July's day short as December,
And with his varying childness cures in me
Thoughts that would thick my blood.

(1.2.165-70)

When we look at soliloquies below, I will share some strategies for breaking down a long speech into smaller units of thought. This strategy can help even with shorter passages such as this one. Note that in form as well as content, these six lines divide neatly into two distinct units of thought, each comprised of three lines ending in a full stop (a period). The first three lines, in which Polixenes lists the various roles his son plays in relation to himself, are linked by the sequence of alliterative sounds in '*my*', '*my m*irth', '*my m*atter', '*my*', '*m*ine', '*my*' and '*my*', as well as the consonance of *s* sounds in 'He*'s*', 'exerci*s*e', '*s*worn', 'para*s*ite', '*s*oldier' and '*s*tatesman'. Linking the two halves of the passage, *s* sounds are also prominent in lines four through six: 'makes', 'July's', 'short', 'December', 'childness', 'cures' and 'Thoughts'. Whereas line one, an extrametrical iambic line, is fairly regular, line two shifts the pattern with an initial trochee ('**Now** my'); the stressed '**Now**' is antithetically answered by the stressed '**then**'. The heavily stressed spondee of '**sworn friend**' gives the *friend* side of the friend-enemy antithesis more importance than the metrically regular *enemy*. In the third line, the sequence of caesurae, building up to the stressed monosyllable '**all**' and the full stop, serves to mark the end of Polixenes' first thought unit: my son is everything to me.

Suggesting the beginning of a new idea, the fourth line, like the first line, is extrametrical; lines one and four even end with the same sound ('Decemb*er*' and 'matt*er*'). The only enjambed line in the speech, the fifth line ends with the speech's only pyrrhic foot ('in me'), the weakness of which pushes the momentum forward to the important word 'Thoughts', which receives additional stress as an initial trochee ('**Thoug**hts that') and is linked through alliteration and stress with '*th*ick' later in the line. Polixenes concludes his second thought – my son gives me joy – with the claim that the boy can cure him of thick thoughts, or melancholy.

While so far we've considered metrical patterns within a single character's speech, characters sometimes share a complete pentameter verse line. In a modern Shakespeare edition, a shared line looks like this on the page:

HERMIONE
   Nay but you will?
POLIXENES
                   I may not, verily.   45

In the eighteenth century, George Steevens was the first editor of Shakespeare to indent the second line to indicate that one character picks up the verse line where the other character leaves off (Rokison 290). In the example above (1.2.45), Hermione delivers the first four syllables of the pentameter line, and Polixenes completes the line with the final six syllables. The number printed in the right margin following Polixenes' words indicates that Hermione's and Polixenes' words collectively make up line 45 of the scene. Although shared lines can serve many functions, including imparting 'fluidity to the dialogue', they might also signal that the speakers are communicating in a particularly intense, connected way, either in concert with or opposition to each other (Rokison 292). According to Russ McDonald, the 'dovetailing of half-lines and even shorter segments makes the dialogue more conversational, less oratorical: characters seem to be talking with one another, not just at one another' (84). The sharing of lines between Hermione and Polixenes might even contribute to Leontes' belief that their relationship is inappropriately close (1.2.108).

Let's consider a final example of the effect of shared lines in heightening the intensity of a conversation. Russ McDonald observes that as 'characters trade off phrases in a rhythmic fashion, the listener may intuit a growing agitation or increasingly intimate engagement' (84). Shakespeare creates an effect of 'growing agitation' near the conclusion of Florizel's argument with his disguised father over his impending marriage to Perdita. When Polixenes insists that Florizel inform his father of his betrothal, Florizel refuses:

> FLORIZEL   I yield all this;
> But for some other reasons, my grave sir,
> Which 'tis not fit you know, I not acquaint
> My father of this business.
> POLIXENES   Let him know't.
> FLORIZEL
>   He shall not.
> POLIXENES
>   Prithee let him.
> FLORIZEL
>   No, he must not.
>   (4.4.415-19)

Maintaining his composure in the face of his unknown guest's importunity, Florizel explains that he has good reasons for hiding his plans from his father. Polixenes takes over the verse line in which Florizel alludes to him, bluntly insisting that Florizel tell his father this important news. Here the conversation picks up speed and heat, as Florizel and Polixenes curtly reiterate their positions in a single verse line divided into three parts: essentially a pattern of no – yes – no. Their mounting frustration and anger are beautifully conveyed by the sense that each man is jumping on the other's words in an effort to convey the urgency of his position.

Soliloquies

We can now apply these strategies for analysing blank verse to a significant dramatic form: the verse soliloquy In a soliloquy, a character expresses private thoughts; theatrical convention holds that if any other characters are present on stage, they are unable to hear this self-directed speech. Some of the most memorable soliloquies are those in which a character confronts some moral, psychological or political dilemma. The soliloquy provides an opportunity to think through the pros and cons of such monumental decisions. For instance, Macbeth ponders the consequences of killing the king, and Hamlet ponders the consequences of killing himself. At other times, a soliloquy gives us access to a character's secret plans: Iago rehearses his scheme to destroy Othello; Richard III plots his rise to the throne; Lady Macbeth prepares herself for regicide. Soliloquies also function as vehicles for emotional expression, as in Macbeth's 'Tomorrow' soliloquy lamenting the futility of life, or in Olivia's shocked discovery in *Twelfth Night* that she has fallen in love with a servant. When analysing a soliloquy, consider what the character accomplishes by pondering a dilemma, confessing to a scheme or expressing an emotion. Has the character made any decisions or come to any conclusions by the end of the soliloquy?

It can be informative to consider who has soliloquies and how they are distributed throughout the play. Remarkably, of the six verse soliloquies in *The Winter's Tale*, four take place in the same scene (1.2). Three of those four are delivered by Leontes and concern Hermione's infidelity: the fourth presents Camillo's private response to Leontes's command that he murder Polixenes. Leontes's fourth and last verse soliloquy in the play expresses his anguished desire to take vengeance against Polixenes and Hermione (2.3). In the play's sixth and last verse soliloquy, Antigonus recounts the disturbing appearance of Hermione's ghost the previous night (3.3). In sum, all of the play's six verse soliloquies take place in the first half of the play and concern the emergence, development and consequences of Leontes's jealousy. *The Winter's Tale* also contains some prose soliloquies: in one, the Shepherd expresses his amazement at having discovered the infant Perdita; in a series of smaller passages, Autolycus reveals his origins, his criminal methods, his plans to rob the shepherds, his success at having done so and his plans to assist Florizel. There are no soliloquies in Act Five. What might be significant about the way that soliloquies are assigned and distributed throughout *The Winter's Tale*? What might it mean, for instance, that no women have soliloquies? Why does Autolycus have so many soliloquies in the few scenes in which he appears? What might these soliloquies tell us about his role in the play? What is the effect of the absence of soliloquies in Act Five?

In the previous chapter, we saw how Leontes's second soliloquy ('Can thy Dam?') proffers, tests and confirms the hypothesis that Hermione's promiscuity is not imaginary but real. Several critics have argued that Leontes's irrational suspicions of adultery are provoked by the highly visible spectacle of Hermione's pregnant body, which provides 'evidence' of her sexual desire and activity (Adelman 220; Bradley and Pollard 256-9; Cavell 209-10; Coldiron 33-6; Duncan 143-5; Enterline 206; Moncrief 35; Parker 183; Robertson 303-4; Traub 44; Wells 249). In his third and longest soliloquy, Leontes finds additional 'evidence' of Hermione's betrayal in the proverbial promiscuity of women: 'Should all despair / That have revolted wives, the tenth of mankind / Would hang themselves' (1.2.197-9). He uses the argumentative form of the soliloquy to reach the seemingly inevitable conclusion of adultery that he has already discovered in his wife's body: 'be it concluded, / No barricado for a belly' (1.2.202-3). If husbands have no way of barricading or preventing unauthorized access to their wives' lustful 'bellies' (i.e. vaginas, and ultimately, wombs), then Hermione must be pregnant with another man's child. A heavy dose of dramatic irony adds poignancy to Leontes's Act One soliloquies. For Leontes, the soliloquy becomes, as it does for Shakespeare's tragic protagonists, a vehicle for thinking through a difficult problem or situation in order to reach a conclusion that seems right or true, even if acting upon it involves risk or pain. In the course of his three soliloquies, Leontes reaches a firm conviction in the truth of Hermione's infidelity – a 'truth' that the play gives us every good reason to believe is a falsehood.

Leontes's assurance at having accurately diagnosed his 'disease' of cuckoldry is bolstered by the soliloquy's strength as a vehicle for logical and rhetorical analysis (1.2.206). To explore what that means, let's take a close look at the structure of Leontes's first soliloquy. We will analyse both the logical process of Leontes's thinking – how he marshals, weighs and draws conclusions from his evidence – and the rhetorical devices that reveal and reinforce the strong feelings he brings to his reflections. When reading a soliloquy, it's helpful to identify a controlling metaphor or image that runs throughout the passage, connecting what might otherwise seem to be loosely related thoughts. For instance, the conceptual backbone of Macbeth's 'Tomorrow, and tomorrow, and tomorrow' soliloquy is, unsurprisingly, the relentless passage of time. Although Leontes's first soliloquy does not announce a central topic quite so explicitly, his meditation on forbidden intimacies does focus throughout on body parts and processes.

Before moving into analysis, it will be helpful to identify some of the common rhetorical devices that Shakespeare used. If the names of these figures sound odd, it is because they derive from ancient Greek teachings on the art of public speaking. Through his rigorous grammar school education, Shakespeare would have learned scores of such figures.

anaphora: repetition of a word/words at the beginning of successive verse lines or clauses.
Ex.: '*But let him* say so then, and let him go; / *But let him* swear so and he shall not stay' (1.2.35-6).

antanaclasis: the repetition of a word using a different meaning of the word.
Ex.: 'Go *play*, boy, play. Thy mother *plays*, and I / *Play* too; but so disgraced a part...' (1.2.186-7).

antimetabole: the repetition of words in successive clauses, in reversed (*a b* / *b a*) order.
Ex.: 'Plainly as *heaven* sees *earth* and *earth* sees *heaven*' (1.2.313).

antithesis: the contrasting of ideas through parallel structure.
Ex.: 'thou met'st with *things dying*, I with *things newborn*' (3.3.110-11).

aposiopesis: breaking off a statement before it is complete.
Ex.: 'We cannot with such magnificence – *in so rare* – *I know not what to say*' (1.1.12-13). The italicized phrases indicate aposiopesis.

asteismus: a witty retort making punning use of another speaker's word or metaphor.
Ex.: 'HERMIONE: you, my lord, / Do but *mistake*. LEONTES: You have *mistook*, my lady, / Polixenes for Leontes' (2.1.80-2).

diacope: repetition of a word separated by one or two intervening words.
Ex.: 'We must be *neat* – not *neat*, but cleanly, captain' (1.2.123).

epizeuxis: repetition of a word or phrase in immediate succession.
Ex.: '*you lie, you lie!*' (1.2.297).
Ex.: 'There is no tongue that moves, *none, none,* i'th'world' (1.2.20).

hyperbole: the use of exaggeration for emphasis.
Ex.: 'A *thousand* knees, / *Ten thousand* years together' (3.2.207-8).

parison: even balance of words in parallel grammatical structures.
Ex.: 'Though I *with death* and *with* / *Reward* did *threaten* and *encourage* him, / *Not doing* it and *being done*' (3.2.160-2).

parenthesis: insertion of words that interrupt the grammatical flow of a sentence.
Ex.: 'The good queen – / *For she is good* – hath brought you forth a daughter' (2.3.63-4).

polyptoton: the repetition of a word in a different case, inflection or voice.
Ex.: 'I may be *negligent, foolish,* and *fearful*; / In every one of these no man is free, / But that his *negligence,* his *folly, fear…*' (1.2.248-50).

It is unnecessary to memorize all these devices, though you might try to memorize one or two of them and jot their names in the margin of your Shakespeare text or reading journal. You can consult this list, as well as others that you might find in books, essays or websites about classical rhetoric, when you recognize that some kind of rhetorical figure is being used but you can't remember what it's called. Even if you can't identify the name of a rhetorical figure while writing about Shakespeare, however, you can always explain in your own words how he is using techniques of repetition, parallelism or patterned rearrangement. The important thing is not that you memorize the name and spelling of each rhetorical device but that you understand and can explain how they convey meaning in particular contexts.

Let's look now at the use of rhetorical figures in Leontes's first soliloquy (1.2.108-19). Below I have reproduced the soliloquy along with Hermione's words immediately preceding it, which, we might note, use parison (rhetorical parallelism) to connect her affection for her 'husband' to her affection for her 'friend' Polixenes. Also note the editorial additions of a stage direction and an aside:

HERMIONE
    The one for ever earned a royal husband;
    Th'other for some while a friend.
     [*Gives her hand to Polixenes.*]
LEONTES [*aside*]   Too hot, too hot!
    To mingle friendship far is mingling bloods.
    I have *tremor cordis* on me. My heart dances,
    But not for joy, not joy. This entertainment
    May a free face put on, derive a liberty
    From heartiness, from bounty, fertile bosom,
    And well become the agent – 't may, I grant –
    But to be paddling palms and pinching fingers,
    As now they are, and making practised smiles
    As in a looking-glass; and then to sigh, as 'twere
    The mort o'th'deer – O, that is entertainment
    My bosom likes not, nor my brows.

                                            (1.2.107-19)

A unifying subject of this soliloquy concerns the bodily interactions of Hermione, Polixenes and Leontes. Its opening line – 'Too hot! Too hot!' – completes extrametrically (with eleven syllables) Hermione's previous line of seven syllables in which she refers to Polixenes as a 'friend': a word that, in this period, could also mean lover. The shared line suggests that Hermione's comparison of husband to friend might immediately provoke Leontes's suspicions of infidelity. 'Too hot! Too hot!' is an instance of epizeuxis (a repeated phrase), which here might convey escalating anxiety or anger at the physical intimacy between Hermione and Polixenes, since 'hot' could mean lusty. For example, Iago describes Desdemona and Cassio in the act of sex as 'hot as monkeys' (*Oth* 3.3.406), and Othello chides Desdemona for her 'hot' hand (3.4.39). In *The Rape of Lucrece*, the rapist Tarquin's 'hot heart' is 'scorch[ed]' by lust (314). But how would Leontes know if his wife and friend had 'hot' hearts – or in a modern idiom, were hot for each other?

Leontes's next observation is less physiological than sociological. 'To mingle friendship far is mingling bloods' is a perfect iambic pentameter sentence, the metrical regularity of which enhances the unquestioned authority of its axiomatic sentiment. It's common knowledge, Leontes affirms, that when affectionate friends 'mingle' too 'far', their intimacy can slide into the sexual 'mingling' of bodily fluids ('bloods') in the act of intercourse. The repetition of 'to mingle' in a different grammatical form ('is mingling') is an example of polyptoton: the shift from the infinitive to the more active present continuous verb conveys Leontes's fear that Hermione has progressed from innocent friendship to active adultery.

Having observed the behaviour of his hot-hearted wife and friend, Leontes diagnoses his own heart with the Latin medical term '*tremor cordis*'. What rhetorical effect does the introduction of Latin produce? Is there any connection between a hot heart and a heart that trembles or 'dances'? Using a double diacope, Leontes clarifies that his heart moves '*not* for *joy*, *not joy*', but neglects to specify what emotion(s) he does feel. Why might that omission be significant? Following 'not for joy, not joy' is a strong medial caesura (a mid-line period) that signals a shift in direction, as Leontes now turns from self-diagnosis punctuated with short sentences to a single long sentence that ponders the meaning of Hermione's behaviour towards Polixenes.

In this next section of the soliloquy, Leontes offers several possible causes for Hermione's warm 'entertainment' of Polixenes. Although he seems to have abandoned diagnosis of interior states for observation of outward behaviours, he continues to focus on body parts, especially the heart: he mentions Hermione's 'face', 'heartiness' and 'bosom'. How is 'heartiness' alike or different from the hot hearts and dancing hearts Leontes has already mentioned? What does Leontes mean by 'fertile bosom'? With a parenthetical interruption – ''t may, I grant' – Leontes concedes that Hermione's behaviour might be innocent. What might the parenthesis reveal about Leontes's state of mind at this pivotal moment in his soliloquy?

The following word 'But' effects an important rhetorical pivot or change of direction. When reading soliloquies, always pay particular attention to words that orient you to the direction of the argument. For instance, 'now' and 'then' orient you to the speaker's sense of time; 'but', 'yet', and 'however' tell you that the speaker is shifting to an antithetical position or circumstance; 'if' and 'then' signal a hypothetical relation of cause and effect; 'thus', 'then', and 'hence' introduce a conclusion or resolution. Leontes's 'But' rescinds his acknowledgement of Hermione's possible innocence. Using alliteration, assonance and parison, Leontes introduces a list of graphic verbs that purport to describe what his wife and friend are doing with their bodies: *p*addling *p*alms, *p*inching fingers, making *p*racticed sm*i*les and s*i*gh[s]. What might this patterning of sounds and grammatical structures reveal about Leontes's emotional state when imagining these activities?

Leontes concludes his soliloquy with a vocative: the sound 'O', which appears frequently in Shakespeare to convey strong emotion. Consider what emotion(s) might be conveyed by the vocative in these lines from other plays: 'O Buckingham, take heed of yonder dog' (*Richard III* 1.3.288); 'O, I am out of breath in this fond chase' (*A Midsummer Night's Dream* 2.2.92); 'O my dear Antonio, / How have the hours racked and tortured me / Since I have lost thee!' (*Twelfth Night* 5.1.214-16); 'O most wicked speed, to post / With such dexterity to incestuous sheets!' (*Hamlet* 1.2.154-5); 'O nation miserable! / With an untitled tyrant bloody-sceptered' (*Macbeth* 4.3.103-4); 'O brave new world / That has such people in't!' (*The Tempest* 5.1.183-4). How would you identify the emotion expressed by Leontes's 'O, that is entertainment / My bosom likes not, nor my brows'? Note how in the process of soliloquizing, Leontes has shifted the referent of the crucial word 'entertainment'. When he reaches the end of the soliloquy, what has 'entertainment' come to mean and what emotional response does it evoke in him? Leontes concludes by returning to an image of his 'bosom' (heart), to which he alliteratively joins an image of the cuckold's 'brows', on which horns, according to folklore, supposedly sprouted to reveal a husband's sexual humiliation. How does Leontes address through this soliloquy the relationship between private feelings (what is hidden in the bosom) and public knowledge (what is visible on the body)?

Hermione's oration

In the first part of *The Winter's Tale*, Leontes has most of the soliloquies, but Hermione takes centre stage in one of only three formal trial scenes in Shakespeare's plays, the others being Antonio's trial in *The Merchant of Venice* and Katherine's trial in *Henry VIII* (Bergeron 4). Hermione's conduct during the trial provides a remarkable illustration of Shakespeare's care in developing characterization through language. In the trial scene (3.2), Hermione appears onstage for the first time since her imprisonment (2.1). At that earlier moment, Hermione had patiently declared her faith that the gods would eventually exonerate her:

> I must be patient till the heavens look
> With an aspect more favourable. Good my lords,
> I am not prone to weeping, as our sex
> Commonly are, the want of which vain dew
> Perchance shall dry your pities; but I have
> That honourable grief lodged here which burns
> Worse than tears drown.
>
> (2.1.106-12)

Rejecting the imagery of liquidity commonly associated with female inconstancy ('weeping', 'dew', 'tears', 'drown'), Hermione worries that her inability to cry will 'dry' the court's pity, but she also insists that her heart 'burns' with inward grief. The caesura following 'favourable' in the second line signals a shift in direct address to the royal advisers ('Good my lords'), to whom Hermione appeals in a long sentence that is almost entirely enjambed, possibly conveying the urgent sincerity of words flowing straight from the heart. As Leontes's 'Too hot!' soliloquy had extrapolated from Hermione's behaviour the lust in her heart, so Hermione insists that the absence of tears on her face should not be interpreted as evidence of guilt; rather, it proves that she possesses a fortitude uncommon in women, an 'honourable grief' that enflames her heart. Following a terminal caesura (a semicolon) in line 110, the turn word 'but' introduces an antithesis between grief that burns and tears that drown.

That Hermione's formal speech or oration during the trial echoes much of the language in this short speech suggests that her traumatic experiences in prison have not shaken her faith in divine providence or her determination to exonerate her honour. Just as Hermione had earlier expressed faith in the 'heavens', so at the outset of her trial she affirms that 'powers divine' will prove her innocence (2.1.112, 3.2.27). Her determination to be 'patient' when remanded to prison is confirmed by her continued 'patience' under duress, which will eventually be justified by the gods (2.1.112, 3.2.31). Nor has her 'honourable grief' abated (2.1.111). Central themes of her oration are the importance of proving her unstained 'honour' to the world and the abiding 'grief' that liberates her from fearing death (3.2.40, 42, 50, 62, 108). In short, whereas the rigors of prison might have made another woman beg for her life, rage against her cruel treatment or even confess to crimes she had not committed in a desperate bid for clemency, Hermione has retained her dignity and mental sharpness. She responds to Leontes's accusations 'with heroic stoicism rather than passion' (Villeponteaux 156). David Bergeron argues that in her defence Hermione deliberately employs, in three distinct stages, the three basic proofs of classical rhetoric: *ethos* (an appeal to the speaker's character, such as establishing credibility or accomplishments), *logos* (the use of logic or reason, such as citing facts) and *pathos* (the attempt to produce in listeners an emotional response, such as pity or outrage). Not only has Hermione given birth in the sub-standard conditions of prison, she has prepared a carefully structured legal defence (Bergeron 5).

Reporting

In the Introduction, we discussed the importance of reported action in *The Winter's Tale* in terms of the kinds of genres or tales embedded in the play: Antigonus tells a 'ghost story' about Hermione (3.3); courtiers share eyewitness accounts of the tragicomic reunion of Perdita and Leontes that has just occurred in a nearby chamber (5.2). In Chapter One we also addressed how *The Winter's Tale* opens with two courtiers reporting the long-standing affection between Leontes and Polixenes as well as the future promise of Mamillius (1.1). A report provides an account of a past event or series of events that we have not witnessed: either something that has just happened 'offstage' (i.e. in the world of the play), such as Antigonus's death, or something that has happened a long time ago or during a long stretch of time, such as the history of the two kings' friendship. Having explored the dramatic functions of soliloquies and oration, let's take a closer look at the dramatic functions of reported action.

The first instance of reporting in *The Winter's Tale*, the courtiers' discussion in 1.1 provides a good example of reporting for the purposes of exposition and foreshadowing. By establishing the childhood friendship of Polixenes and Leontes, this discussion allows us to speculate about the rivalry between the kings – who are as close as 'twins' (1.2.67) – as a possible cause of Leontes's jealousy, and also heightens the tragedy of the loss of such a lifelong bond. 'The heavens continue their loves', says Camillo in a prayer that, as we will soon discover, goes unfulfilled (1.1.31). Once aware of Leontes's jealousy, Polixenes recognizes that Leontes's anger will be in proportion to the affection and longevity of their friendship, Polixenes being 'a man which *ever* / Professed [love] to him' (1.2.451-2; emphasis added). Camillo's report of the 'interchange of gifts, letters, loving embassies' between the kings provides a material history for the profession of love that has 'ever' bound the two men (1.1.28). In narrating how Leontes and Polixenes share a past, the courtiers also establish the thematic importance of time in the play.

A different kind of report lightens the tragedy of offstage deaths in 3.3, and thus provides a fulcrum between the tragic and comic halves of the play. The Clown has witnessed the mariners' deaths in a shipwreck and Antigonus's death at the claws of a bear. Pragmatically, the Clown's report removes the difficulty of having to depict these deaths on stage, particularly since theatrical props, sets and visual effects were extremely minimal in Shakespeare's time. Dramatically, the Clown's report leavens the sadness we might feel at these deaths through the homeliness of its images and haphazardness of its organization:

> O, the most piteous cry of the poor souls! Sometimes to see 'em, and not to see 'em; now the ship boring the moon with her mainmast, and anon swallowed with yeast and froth, as you'd thrust a cork into a hogshead. And then for the land-service, to see how the bear tore out his shoulder-bone, how he cried to me

for help, and said his name was Antigonus, a nobleman! But to make an end of the ship – to see how the sea flapdragoned it! But first, how the poor souls roared, and the sea mocked them, and how the poor gentleman roared, and the bear mocked him, both roaring louder than the sea or weather.

(3.3.88-99)

As with other prose passages in *The Winter's Tale*, the Clown's speech is not artless. He uses rhetorical devices such as antithesis ('to see 'em' / 'not to see 'em'), metaphor (the ship in the ocean as a cork bobbing in a cask of ale), parison ('the sea mocked them' / 'the bear mocked him'; 'the poor souls roared' / 'the poor gentleman roared') and polyptoton ('roared' / 'roaring'). Despite these rhetorical patterns, however, the speech's lack of logical progression gives it a loose or scattered feel. For instance, instead of signalling a sharp turn in the argument, the Clown's use of 'but' keeps shifting our focus from one event to another in a dizzying manner: he describes the shipwreck '[a]nd then' turns to the mauling of Antigonus, 'but' returns to the shipwreck, 'but first' reports how the mariners roared 'and' how Antigonus roared 'and' how the bear roared. This stylistic disorganization draws attention to the surface of the Clown's report – its linguistic patterns and shuttling rhythms – instead of to the tragic, gruesome events being reported. The incongruity between the speech's style and content becomes a source of dark humour, and thus makes a fitting transition to the lighter, more comic, second part of the play.

Conversely, the courtiers who narrate the reunion of Perdita and Leontes describe it as a joyous event haunted by regret and sorrow (5.2). It is generally assumed that Shakespeare decided not to stage this reunion so as to reserve for the play's emotional climax the animation of Hermione's statue in the following scene. Whereas in the Introduction we analysed the reunion scene in terms of its generic traits as a tragicomic mixture of joy (at Perdita's return) and sorrow (at the remembered loss of Hermione), here we will address the dramatic effects of reporting. The report of the revelation of Perdita's identity and subsequent reunion with her father unfolds in several stages as news of this event travels from the privacy of the king's chamber to the ears of the general public. An initial sense of privacy is created by the Gentleman's report that various onlookers were 'commanded out of the chamber' right after the old shepherd confessed to having discovered the infant Perdita (5.2.5-6). Rendered speechless, Leontes and Camillo communicate their wonder through 'dumbness' (silence) and 'gesture' (13-14). With Rogero's entrance, the focus shifts from the private and silent 'passion of wonder' to public manifestations of joy at the spreading 'news' of Perdita's return (16, 27).

As the news spreads, however, we are reminded of how Leontes's past crimes continue to impact the present. While reporting the 'proofs' that 'the king's daughter is found', Paulina's Steward recalls the deaths of Hermione and Antigonus (23): the infant Perdita had been abandoned wrapped in a 'mantle of Queen Hermione's' and accompanied with letters composed by Antigonus, whose violent death is confirmed by the return of his handkerchief and rings (32-3). Despite the joyful reunion between the two kings, Leontes, 'as if that joy were now become a loss', laments Hermione's death and asks Polixenes's forgiveness (49-50). The court also learns of the mariners' death, 'so that all the instruments which aided to expose the child were even then lost when it was found' (69-71). Overjoyed by Perdita's return and saddened by her husband's fate, Paulina has one eye 'declined' to the earth in mourning, and one eye 'elevated' to the heavens in celebration of the oracle's fulfilment (73-4). This scene of prose reporting thus rehearses as a tragic 'old tale' the events of the first part of the play: Leontes's jealousy, Perdita's banishment, and the deaths of Hermione, Antigonus and the mariners (60). We are not allowed to forget the terrible price of Perdita's survival. These reports prepare us for the play's finale not only by explaining the putative origin of Hermione's statue, but by reminding us that this incredible work of art is merely a substitute for the living woman who, like Perdita, has been absent for the past sixteen years.

Writing matters

This section gives you the opportunity to explore through writing the topics addressed in this chapter: prose and verse as the basic mediums of dramatic speech; soliloquy as a form of expression that gives us access to a character's active thought process; rhetorical devices and appeals as methods of persuasion; and reporting as a strategy for providing information about what has happened offstage or in the past, as well as for shaping our perspectives on and emotional responses to such events.

Alternating prose and verse

As we have seen, shifts from prose to verse (or vice versa) within or between scenes might signal a change in mood, setting or characterization. The alternating of prose and verse in the sheep-shearing scene (4.4) gives texture to the various events that transpire during this extremely long episode. For this exercise, identify any one instance of a shift from prose to verse or from verse to prose in 4.4 and discuss its significance. Some issues you might want to address in your analysis: How might a reader or audience member register this shift from prose to verse or from verse to prose? What are the effects of this shift for you as a reader or as an (imagined) audience member? What kind of changes does the change in medium signal or emphasize? Despite the change in medium, are there any continuities (in topic, language, tone etc.) between the section in prose and the section in verse? In other words, might we wish to avoid the implication that a shift from one speech style to another necessarily accompanies a complete change in direction or tone?

The art of prose

As we have seen, the distinction between verse and prose does not correspond to a distinction between artful and artless language. Prose can be rhetorically patterned, rich with figures of speech and emotionally compelling. For this exercise, analyse Autolycus's prose soliloquy in 4.4.674-86, explaining how his language conveys his attitudes or feelings about his profession as a thief. Some issues you might want to address in your analysis: What rhetorical devices can you identify and what is their effect? Are any of Autolycus's words particularly significant in terms of their connotations or imagery? Can you detect a logical progression in Autolycus's thinking from the beginning to the end of his soliloquy? What is the dramatic purpose or importance of this soliloquy?

The art of verse

Scholars have observed changes in how Shakespeare composed verse as he became a more experienced dramatist. According to Russ McDonald, 'Shakespeare's blank verse develops over the course of his career from regular to irregular, from smooth to rough, from rhythmically simple to rhythmically various' (89). McDonald offers six examples of this more 'irregular', 'rough' and 'various' style in the late romances: (1) extrametrical lines; (2) feminine endings; (3) short phrases or segmented lines; (4) terminal caesurae; (5) frequent trochaic or spondaic feet; (6) enjambment. (If you need a reminder of what these terms mean, review pp. 73-4 above). In this writing exercise, analyse the following passage, observing where each of these six stylistic traits appears and explaining how they contribute to the meaning or impact of the passage.

> LEONTES
> She I killed? I did so. But thou strik'st me
> Sorely, to say I did; it is as bitter
> Upon thy tongue as in my thought. Now, good now,
> Say so but seldom.
> (5.1.17-20)

The impact of songs

In his edition of *The Winter's Tale*, John Pitcher includes and provides a comprehensive discussion of the music that might have been used for Autolycus's Act Four songs in original performances of the play. We don't know for certain what vocal or instrumental music seventeenth-century audiences might have heard in performances of *The Winter's Tale*, although in the cases of 'Jog on' and 'Get you hence' there is a 'good chance' that the experts' theories are correct (Pitcher 385). In any case, Pitcher provides his and other scholars' best educated guesses regarding the contemporary musical settings that would have been used for the songs 'When daffodils begin to peer' (4.3.1-12), 'But shall I go mourn?' (4.3.15-22) 'Jog on, jog on, the footpath way' (4.3.122-5), 'Get you hence' (4.4.298-313) and 'Will you buy any tape?'

(4.4.320-8), as well as the 'dance of satyrs' (396-404). If you have some knowledge of music, you might enjoy this exercise: analyse the music of one of Autolycus's songs, explaining how the music enhances the verbal text. Depending on the extent of your musical knowledge, you might address any musical elements you find significant, such as time signature, rhythmic patterns, voice leading, chord progression, accidentals and so on. The purpose of this exercise is not simply to analyse musical form, however, but to explain how the music contributes to the meaning of the song, with 'meaning' understood to encompass not only the connotations of the verbal text, but also the possible visceral/emotional impact of hearing live music. Some issues you might wish to address: what does the music contribute to the characterization of Autolycus? How does the music affect the mood of a particular scene or episode? What important subjects or ideas does the music bring out or emphasize in the lyrics? Especially when you consider that the Sicily of Acts One through Three is without music, how does music contribute to Shakespeare's representation of Bohemia in Act Four?

Analysing soliloquies

In this chapter we used various techniques to explicate Leontes's soliloquies. This exercise asks you to apply the same techniques to the soliloquy in which Camillo ponders Leontes's command to murder Polixenes (1.2.348-60). Addressing such elements as rhetorical devices, logical argumentation or variations in metrical patterns, show how Camillo's soliloquy leads him to the conclusion that escape is his only option. Some issues you might wish to address in your analysis: What is the significance of the 'O' that opens the soliloquy? How do caesurae, end-stopped or enjambed lines, extrametrical lines or length of sentences contribute to the import or emotional impact of Camillo's words? What rhetorical devices are present in the soliloquy and what do they convey about Camillo's thoughts and feelings? How do words like 'but', 'if', 'since', or 'let' help us follow the progress of his thoughts? Which individual words seem particularly significant in giving us insight into Camillo's feelings, beliefs or values?

Analysing Hermione's oration

When discussing Hermione's long speech of self-defence above, I noted David Bergeron's argument that Hermione employs the three basic proofs of classical rhetoric: *ethos* (an appeal to the speaker's character, such as their credibility or accomplishments), *logos* (the use of logic or reason, such as citing facts) and *pathos* (the attempt to produce an emotional response in listeners). Bergeron divides Hermione's speech into three sections in which she employs ethos (3.2.21-53), then logos (60-75) and finally pathos (89-114). For this exercise, choose *one* of these three sections and show how Hermione appeals to ethos, logos or pathos in it, respectively. If you choose the first section, explain how Hermione attempts to establish her virtuous character in order to earn credibility with her audience. If you choose the second section, explain which facts or pieces of evidence Hermione cites to prove her innocence. If you choose the third section, discuss how Hermione uses language aimed to generate certain emotions in her audience. Should you wish, you are also free to argue that the strategies of ethos, logos and pathos do not map onto these three sections of Hermione's speech as neatly as Bergeron suggests. For instance, you might argue that even if in the first part of her speech Hermione appeals largely to ethos, she also appeals to pathos (and demonstrate how).

Reporting

In this chapter, we considered the dramatic function of reporting in 5.2, the long prose scene in which court observers describe the emotional reactions attending the discovery of Perdita's identity. For this writing exercise, imagine that you are directing a stage production of *The Winter's Tale*. You decide that the characters who are absent from this scene in the text of the play – the Shepherd, Leontes, Camillo, Polixenes, Perdita, Florizel and Paulina – will silently perform the facial expressions and bodily gestures attributed to them by the speaking characters. The speaking actors will be located near the back of the stage; the silent ones at the front, so the audience can clearly see them. First, choose *one* of the following passages: 5.2.3-19, 5.2.39-55 or 5.2.71-87. Next, describe in your own words how the language of the passage not only offers an account of what characters are literally doing (e.g. staring, embracing, lifting their hands) but also suggests specific emotional colourings to those actions. Explain how your silent actors will perform these actions so as to convey those emotions to the audience. For instance, you might describe whether the actors are standing, kneeling or sitting; whether they are close together or far apart; what kinds of facial expressions they wear; how their heads, arms or legs are positioned in relation to each other; how they might make physical contact with each other; what kind of clothing they are wearing; or any other detail that might convey their emotional states as you interpret them based on the courtiers' reports.

3

Language and history

A four-hundred-year-old play inevitably confronts us with unfamiliar concepts and perspectives. Learning more about the possible meanings available to original audiences of *The Winter's Tale* opens up avenues for interpretation by helping us to understand how Shakespeare's language addresses contentious issues in his culture. In this chapter we will explore how the language of the play engages contemporary debates about female authority, monarchical politics, festive play and religious devotion. Seventeenth-century English audiences, no less than twenty-first-century audiences, wouldn't have had uniform views on these subjects. Nonetheless, original audiences of *The Winter's Tale* shared certain points of reference for such subjects that would have shaped their responses to the play. We will explore how *The Winter's Tale* complexly engages these subjects by juxtaposing select episodes from the play with contemporary texts, including sermons, conduct manuals, political treatises, anti-theatrical attacks and religious polemics.

Women's speech and authority

In Chapter One, we addressed how the erotic charge traditionally attributed to women's speech might have sparked Leontes's jealousy. As Peter Stallybrass argues, the early modern 'surveillance of women' concentrated upon 'the mouth, chastity, and the threshold of the house', areas which 'were frequently collapsed into each other' (126). In theory, patriarchal governance required women to be silent, sexually pure and contained within the household. Women's speech was frequently connected to their sexual availability, such that 'the closed mouth' becomes 'a sign of chastity' (Stallybrass 127).

Although Leontes does not explicitly accuse Hermione of unchaste speech, he does link Paulina's audacious speech to disobedience and sexual impropriety. In *The Taming of the Shrew*, Katherina's outspokenness earns her the label of 'shrew': a loud and aggressive, and thus evidently unmarriageable, woman. As Lynda Boose argues, *The Taming of the Shrew* alludes to the custom of punishing outspoken women with instruments such as the cucking stool or scold's bridle. Although noblewomen were exempt from such brutal punishments, Leontes's angry denunciation of Paulina's speech alludes to these communal shaming rituals. Despite cultural norms of female silence and obedience, however, early modern women were not always reproved for bold speech and behaviour, as suggested by the saying 'better a shrew than a sheep' (Brown 8). Paulina is certainly no sheep, but is she a shrew? Does Shakespeare's portrayal of Paulina endorse or refute that saying? Is Paulina admirable despite or even because of her outspokenness?

Paulina herself acknowledges her capacity to speak boldly. Analysing the very first lines that a character speaks in a play can give us insight into their beliefs, values or temperament. Paulina's first lines are addressed to a servant: 'The keeper of the prison, call to him. / Let him have knowledge who I am' (2.2.1-2). What is the tone of Paulina's words? What information about Paulina's personality might be conveyed in the first line through its regular iambic meter, caesura after 'prison', and end-stopped line, or through the second line's initial trochee (**Let** him)? Reflecting on Leontes's imprisonment of Hermione, Paulina complains,

> These dangerous, unsafe lunes i'th'king, beshrew them!
> He must be told on't, and he shall. The office
> Becomes a woman best; I'll take't upon me.
> If I prove honey-mouthed, let my tongue blister
> And never to my red-looked anger be
> The trumpet any more.
>
> (2.2.29-34)

'Lunes' means lunacy, because the moon (Latin: *luna*) was believed to cause neurological and mental illnesses. Since 'beshrew' derives from 'shrew' – 'a mischievous or vexatious person' or 'a woman given to railing or scolding' (*OED* shrew, *n*.2, 1.a, 3.a) – that word might reflect Paulina's determination to diagnose or cure the king's madness with harsh language. When Paulina accepts this task as a 'woman', is she suggesting that because women are generally more shrewish than men, she will be able to make Leontes listen to her? Is she invoking the 'scold's privilege': women's freedom of 'uttering truths no one else dare voice' (Jardine 117-8)? Is she suggesting that a woman is the person most qualified to defend another woman's honour, or that a woman is most likely to convince a father to accept an infant daughter as his own child?

Whatever she means, Paulina refuses to be 'honey-mouthed' when confronting the king. Editor John Pitcher glosses 'honey-mouthed' as 'a sweet-talking flatterer' (32n). In *King Lear*, Lear's eldest daughters flatter their father in exchange for material rewards. Instead of trying to moderate their masters' passions, which would risk chastisement, flatterers use their 'glib and oily art' to 'smooth every passion' of their masters, bringing 'oil to fire, snow to their colder moods' (*KL* 1.1.226, 2.2.79). How does the description of flattery as 'oily' or 'smooth' compare to Paulina's image of the 'honey-mouthed' flatterer? What would a honey-mouthed person look or sound like? Paulina imagines the punishment for being honey-mouthed as a blistered tongue, which could no longer serve as 'trumpet' to her 'red-faced anger'. Pitcher explains the military metaphor: a trumpeter 'sounded the arrival of a herald in a red uniform bringing messages from an enemy camp' (33-4n). What are the implications of Paulina imagining her tongue as a battlefield trumpet that expresses 'red-faced anger'?

Having committed to confront Leontes, Paulina calls upon her 'boldness': 'I'll use that tongue I have. If wit flow from't / As boldness from my bosom,... / I shall do good' (51-3). Like 'affection', which we explored in Chapter One, 'bold' and its variants might be considered keywords of the play. What might 'boldness' mean as a quality of Paulina's heart ('bosom') that motivates her tongue? Polixenes claims that had he and Leontes remained innocent boys, they would have 'answered heaven / Boldly, "not guilty"' to the charge of original sin (1.2.73-4). What attitude does Polixenes's 'boldly' convey? What behaviours or qualities does Leontes attribute to Hermione when he describes her entertainment of Polixenes as 'boldness' or claims that she merits the 'bold'st' slanders for committing adultery, which is one of the 'bolder' vices (1.2.183, 2.1.93, 3.2.54)? When Paulina brands Leontes a 'tyrant', a Lord scolds her for the 'boldness' of her speech (3.2.215). Whereas all of these instances appear in the first part of the play, the final appearance of 'bold' is during the sheep-shearing festival, when Perdita names 'bold oxlips' among the flowers that she lacks (4.4.125). In what sense might flowers be described as bold?

Having considered these multiple occurrences of 'bold', we can better understand the paradox of Paulina's confidence in her witty tongue and bold bosom. According to the *OED*, 'bold' during Shakespeare's time could mean '[s]tout-hearted, courageous, daring, fearless'; however, '[i]n a bad sense', it could mean '[a]udacious, presumptuous, too forward' (*OED*, bold *adj*. 1.a, 4.a). Early modern women who were bold in the first, usually positive, sense – daring or fearless – risked being considered bold in the second, negative, sense: audacious or immodest, particularly in the linked realms of speech and sexuality.

Paulina's confrontation of Leontes in 2.3 raises just such questions about the moral character of outspoken women. Complaining about Paulina's 'noise' and 'audacious' behaviour, Leontes links transgressions of speech, gender and sexuality (2.3.38, 41). He derides Paulina as a 'mankind' (masculine, mannish) 'witch' and 'intelligencing bawd': a sexual procuress who presumably carried secret messages between Hermione and Polixenes (2.3.66-7). Witches used curses or spells to harm their enemies and were believed to perform perverse sexual acts with the devil or with their familiars (demonic pets). Leontes also berates Antigonus for failing to 'rule' his wife's tongue (2.3.45). When Paulina objects that Antigonus would have no reason to restrain her honourable behaviour, Antigonus praises her independent judgement: 'La you now, you hear, / When she will take the rein I let her run, / But she'll not stumble' (2.3.49-51). Consider how Antigonus's equine metaphor compares to the use of animal imagery in a contemporary misogynist satire, Joseph Swetnam's *Arraignment of Women* (1615):

> The lion being bitten with hunger, the bear being robbed of her young one, the viper being trod on, all these are nothing so terrible as the fury of a woman. A buck may be enclosed in a park, a bridle rules a horse, a wolf may be tied, a tiger may be tamed: but a froward [difficult] woman will never be tamed, no spur will make her go, nor no bridle will hold her back.
>
> (2)

How would you describe the tone of this passage, especially when compared with Antigonus's equine metaphor? Tellingly, Leontes also uses animal metaphors to shame Antigonus for failing to control his wife: 'Give her the bastard, / Thou dotard; thou art woman-tired, unroosted / By thy Dame Partlet' (3.2.72-4). Because a falcon used its beak to 'tire' or rend its prey, 'woman-tired' means shredded by a woman's mouth. 'Dame Partlet' was a name traditionally applied to a hen, in this case one that has 'unroosted' or driven its mate from its perch (*OED*, Partlet, *n.1*). What is the effect of the king's describing Paulina, a noblewoman, with this kind of language? Why does Leontes insult not only Paulina, but Antigonus?

Leontes connects Paulina's unruly speech both to her gender and to the presumed disorder of her marriage: she is a 'callat' (a whore or scold) of 'boundless tongue, who late hath beat her husband, / And now baits me!' (2.3.89-91). Consider Leontes's claim that Paulina beats her husband in light of puritan minister William Whately's condemnation of wicked wives, who

> chase and scold with their husbands, and rail upon them, and revile them, and shake them together with such terms and carriage, as were unsufferable towards a servant. Stains of womankind, blemishes of their sex, monsters in natures, botches [blemishes] of human society, rude, graceless, impudent, next to harlots, if not the same with them. Let such words leave a blister behind them, and let the canker eat out these tongues.
>
> (39)

For Whately, how does verbal abuse become almost a kind of physical abuse? What language does Whately uses to express his disdain for scolding wives? To return to the play, Leontes's clever pun connects Paulina's 'beating' of her husband with her 'baiting' or tormenting of Leontes. 'Baiting' means setting on dogs to bite other animals for entertainment, as in the contemporary sports of bear-baiting and bull-baiting (*OED* bait, *v*. 1.a, 2.a, 3.a). If Paulina is the dog who bites Leontes, is Antigonus the instigator of his wife's violence? What kind of domestic life is Leontes imagining for this couple? Antigonus refutes Leontes's charge that he is 'worthy to be hanged' for failing to silence his wife: 'Hang all the husbands / That cannot do that feat, you'll leave yourself / Hardly one subject'

(2.3.107-10). What is the basis of Antigonus's self-defence? What is he saying about married life?

As we have seen, early moderns might have regarded a bold woman as admirably courageous or rudely presumptuous. Paulina's language supplies evidence for either case. Supporting the former view, Paulina insists that honour motivates her boldness. Maggie Ellen Ray argues that Paulina, as a 'queen-proxy', takes on the jailed Hermione's former political role (257). Paulina pleads for Leontes to recognize her virtuous intentions:

> Good my liege, I come –
> And I beseech you hear me, who professes
> Myself your loyal servant, your physician,
> Your most obedient counsellor; yet that dares
> Less appear so in comforting your evils
> Than such as most seem yours – I say, I come
> From your good queen.
>
> (2.3.51-7)

In the long parenthesis between the dashes, notice the multiple roles that Paulina assumes in relation to her monarch. What might a king expect of a 'loyal servant', 'physician' or 'obedient counsellor'? The 'yet' following the caesura in line 54 qualifies what Paulina means by 'obedient counsellor'. According to Paulina, how should a truly obedient counsellor advise the king? What should an obedient counsellor 'dare' to do? By contrast, what does Paulina observe about those counsellors who only 'seem' obedient to Leontes?

It is also possible to argue that Paulina is rudely presumptuous in her behaviour towards the king. She pronounces him 'ignorant', 'mad' and a 'traitor' for having betrayed the honour of the royal family (2.3.69-70). Aiming to prove Leontes's paternity of his daughter, Paulina observes that the more that the girl resembles her 'unworthy' and 'unnatural' father, the worse off she will be (2.3.111). Paulina warns Leontes that his 'weak-hinged' delusions will make him 'ignoble' and 'scandalous' to others (2.3.117-19). How, if at all, do these insults correspond with Paulina's adoption of the roles of 'loyal servant', 'physician' and 'obedient counsellor' to her king? What kinds of risks does Paulina take in addressing her king so sharply, and what makes her willing to take such risks? Do her barbs have a beneficial purpose, or are they just an expression of her 'red-looked anger' (2.2.33)? For some critics, Paulina's behaviour towards Leontes in the wake of Hermione's apparent death is 'frighteningly harsh and manipulative' (McCoy 138). Do you agree? Does she go too far in castigating her king?

Obedience and resistance

The conflict between Paulina and Leontes is informed not only by early modern gender ideology but by political ideology, that is, by contested ideas about the duties and privileges of subjects and monarchs. Through the arguments between Leontes and his courtiers, particularly Camillo, Antigonus and Paulina, *The Winter's Tale* puts into circulation a host of terms that are central to seventeenth-century debates about the powers and limits of monarchical authority, including 'counsel', 'service', 'obedience', 'rebellion', 'prerogative' and 'tyranny'. As king, Leontes cannot be 'compelled' by his subjects to listen to reason, as Paulina bitterly observes (2.3.89). If the monarch is at the pinnacle of the social hierarchy, then who has the right to intervene when a monarch acts unreasonably? What are the limits of resistance to monarchical power (Styrt 390-2)?

Camillo plays the role of counsellor and loyal servant throughout the play, first to Leontes and then to Polixenes (Schalkwyk, *Shakespeare* 263-6). Although he has long relied on Camillo's good advice, Leontes faults Camillo for his evident silence about Hermione's adultery:

> I have trusted thee, Camillo,
> With all the nearest things to my heart, as well
> My chamber-counsels, wherein, priest-like, thou
> Has cleansed my bosom; I from thee departed
> Thy penitent reformed. But we have been
> Deceived in thy integrity, deceived
> In that which seems so.
>
> (1.2.233-9)

Leontes has opened up his inmost 'heart' to Camillo, profiting from his wisdom and guidance like a sinner who confesses to and receives absolution ('cleans[ing]') from a 'priest'. Leontes anticipates

Paulina's complaint, quoted above, that those counsellors who 'most seem' loyal might not be so (2.3.56). Whereas Leontes has previously 'trusted' Camillo like a spiritual counsellor, he now claims to have exposed the lie of Camillo's 'integrity'. By failing to reveal Hermione's adultery to him, Leontes reasons, Camillo has shown himself to be dishonest, negligent, foolish or cowardly.

Wise sovereigns will attempt to distinguish honest from dishonest counsellors; the problem in this instance is that Leontes accuses Camillo of disloyalty without credible evidence. Admitting that even the wisest counsellor might occasionally fail to execute his duties through negligence, fear or folly, Camillo reasonably observes that he cannot defend his actions until he knows how, exactly, he has failed. When Leontes challenges him to deny his knowledge of Hermione's infidelity, Camillo begins to push back against his monarch's wild surmises, taking up again the role of the truth-speaking counsellor from whom Leontes has often gleaned wisdom (Kurland 368-70). As Paulina will do later, Camillo diagnoses Leontes's jealousy as a 'dangerous' and 'diseased opinion' and flatly denies the truth of his claims. Just as Leontes will attack Paulina as a 'gross hag' (2.3.106), he insults Camillo as a 'gross lout', 'mindless slave' and 'hovering temporizer' (1.2.299-300). All three insults undercut Camillo's status as a royal adviser. The antithesis of a cultivated courtier is a 'gross lout', an ignorant bumpkin or clown (*OED* lout, *n.1* 1). 'Mindless slave' reduces Camillo's service to the crown to its most abject form. A 'hovering temporizer' is a 'time-server': a courtier who serves whatever ruler or faction is in power at the time, whether 'good' or 'evil', for his own gain (1.2.301). In short, according to Leontes, if Camillo doesn't believe his accusations, he is a stupid, unthinking, hypocritical servant – clearly not a man who can be trusted to advise a king. Commanding Camillo to poison Polixenes, Leontes offers him an ultimatum: 'Do't, and thou hast the one half of my heart; / Do't not, thou splitt'st thine own' (1.2.345-6). Leontes's use of anaphora ('Do't' / 'Do't') and antithesis ('Do't and thou hast' / 'Do't not, thou splittest') makes Camillo's fate seem inevitable: he can only be saved or damned. At this moment, how is Leontes using his power as a sovereign?

Although Camillo agrees to murder Polixenes, he privately determines that the only safe course is to disobey the king's command and flee Sicily. The very belief in the sacredness of kings that requires his 'obedience' to Leontes makes it impossible to murder Polixenes, another 'anointed' king (1.2.351, 355). Anointing refers to the practice of pouring oil on kings' heads 'as a sacred rite' at royal coronation ceremonies (*OED*, anointed, *adj.* 1). When Camillo describes regicide as a damnable sin, he articulates an orthodox royalist belief. For instance, in his political treatise *The True Law of Free Monarchies* (1598), King James – the ruling English monarch when Shakespeare wrote *The Winter's Tale* – claims that subjects can never have a legitimate reason to 'rebel, control, and displace, or cut off their King at their own pleasure' (sig. D5r). Far from 'relieving the commonwealth out of distress', rebellion would only 'heap double distress and desolation upon it' (sig. D6r). By the same logic, even as Camillo refuses to kill Polixenes, he also does not seek to kill Leontes or to conspire with Polixenes, in King James's words, to 'control' or 'displace' his king. Drawing on the familiar analogy of the king as father to his subjects, King James asks, 'Yea, suppose the father were furiously following his sons with a drawn sword: is it lawful for them to turn, and strike again, or make any resistance but by flight' (sig. D4r-v)? Why is the analogy between king and father so useful for monarchial ideology? By making 'resistance but by flight', Camillo resembles the sons in James's metaphor. What are the political consequences of Camillo's passive resistance to his king? In fleeing Sicily, does he act ethically? Does he act for his own benefit, for the benefit of the kingdom, or both?

Although Camillo flees, other counsellors remain to divert Leontes from his disastrous course. Antigonus, supported by other Lords, urges Leontes to consider the terrible consequences of imprisoning Hermione:

Be certain what you do, sir, lest your justice
Prove violence, in the which three great ones suffer:
Yourself, your queen, your son.

(2.1.127-9)

Once again King James provides a royalist context for Antigonus's politically astute warning. As God's representative on earth, King James argues, a king is bound to execute the nation's laws and to punish those who break them; he has the power to 'judge' his subjects, 'but to be judged only by God' (sigs. C5r-v). In other words, the king is the supreme dispenser of both *justice* and of judicial *violence*: the lawful punishment of those who threaten the 'weal, and flourishing of his people' (sig. B4r). When Antigonus warns Leontes that his 'justice' might prove 'violence', he isn't naively denying the necessity of judicial violence; he is suggesting that Leontes's particular kind of justice – 'your justice' – might be *unjust violence* instead of *true justice*. Such violence would harm the royal family and the kingdom. The enjambment in line 127 drives the word 'justice' forward into the next line, where it is quickly revealed to 'prove violence'. Antigonus, like Camillo earlier and Paulina later, risks the king's displeasure by insisting that in defending Hermione he and his companions are providing the good counsel that Leontes requires: 'It is for you we speak, not for ourselves' (2.1.140).

Rejecting this counsel, Leontes attempts to silence his advisers by articulating a theory of absolutist rule. The political situation in *The Winter's Tale* does not precisely reflect that of Shakespeare's England, which was not an absolute but a constitutional monarchy, meaning that the king was bound to follow the common law when ruling on matters of property and liberty that were clearly spelled out therein (Burgess 211-12). Moreover, laws were created not by the king but by Parliament, which was divided into a House of Commons (comprised of elite citizens and knights) and a House of Lords (comprised of noblemen and bishops). In constitutionalist theory, the monarch's rule 'was enhanced and made possible by the counsel and consent' of Parliament (Jordan 18). Despite its importance, Parliament was not an independently functioning institution; the monarch could summon or dissolve it at will. The monarch and Parliament had crucial and mutually sustaining roles in national government.

The difference between the constitutional monarchy of England and the absolute monarchy of Sicily in *The Winter's Tale* is illustrated by Leontes's unilateral imprisonment and trial of Hermione and by his insistence on the royal 'prerogative' that ensures his freedom of action:

> LEONTES   Why, what need we
> Commune with you of this, but rather follow
> Our forceful instigation? Our prerogative
> Calls not your counsels, but our natural goodness
> Imparts this; which if you, or stupefied
> Or seeming so in skill, cannot or will not

Relish a truth like us, inform yourselves
We need no more of your advice.

(2.1.161-8)

Leontes affirms his right to 'follow' no other counsel but his own 'forceful instigation', which suggests that he is influenced less by his reason than by the violent 'urging, spurring, or setting on' of his passions (*OED* instigation, *n.* a). Royal 'prerogative' was the 'special right or privilege exercised by a monarch over all other persons' (*OED* prerogative *n.* 2.a). In England, King James used his prerogative to exercise many powers independently of Parliament and the written law. King James claimed that 'the King is above the law, as both the author, and the giver of strength thereto'; nonetheless, a 'good King' will not only 'rule his subjects by the Law; but even will conform himself in his own actions thereunto' (sig. D1v). In other words, subjects must rely on the king's willingness to rule justly, not on his accountability to the law. King James, of course, represents himself as the 'good king' who rules by law even though he does not have to. Such a position did not sit well in a constitutional monarchy such as England (Kurland 367-8; Lim, 'Prerogative' 28-30; Strain 569-73). Leontes makes the similar claim that his 'natural goodness', not legal constraint, prompts him to seek the wisdom of his counsellors. How are counsellors to respond when the king claims that he alone possesses the truth?

Leontes's arguments with Camillo and Antigonus escalate the courtiers' concerns about his abuse of royal power, culminating in Paulina's references to tyranny. Like 'prerogative', 'tyranny' was an inflammatory concept in early modern political theory. A tyrant was usually defined as an illegitimate monarch (one who seized power unjustly) or as a legitimate monarch who 'put his own interests above those of his subjects (and therefore tended to abuse them)' (Jordan 17). Shakespeare's most notorious tyrants are Richard III and Macbeth, both of whom use treachery and violence to usurp the throne and to advance their own interests. Because they were not beholden to written laws or to legislative institutions such as Parliament, absolute monarchs, in the minds of some political thinkers, were apt to tyrannical abuses of power (Jordan 17). Paulina hints at this danger when she laments that Leontes 'cannot be compelled' to change his false opinion of Hermione (2.3.87). Absolutism contains no mechanism to force the monarch to behave in accordance with what is just or right. Later, Paulina explicitly evokes tyranny:

> I'll not call you tyrant;
> But this most cruel usage of your queen,
> Not able to produce more accusation
> Than your own weak-hinged fancy, something savours
> Of tyranny
>
> (2.3.114-18)

Paulina treads a fine line by not directly calling Leontes a tyrant, but only claiming that his cruel treatment of Hermione 'savours of' (smells of) tyranny. Since tyrants were often associated with cruel tortures and executions, Leontes responds that were he truly a tyrant, he would execute Paulina for her seditious speech. Does Leontes make a reasonable point? What do you make of the fact that he does not, in fact, punish Paulina but merely commands that she be removed from his presence?

It is not until Hermione's trial that the label of 'tyrant' gets definitively attached to Leontes. This is not surprising given that despite promising a 'just and open trial' (2.3.203), Leontes clearly has already determined Hermione's guilt. Hermione asserts that if she is convicted solely on the testimony of Leontes's jealousy, the sentence will be 'rigour', or cruelty, and not 'law' (3.2.112). Apollo's oracle effectively decides the trial by declaring Hermione 'chaste' and Leontes 'a jealous tyrant' (3.2.131). The qualifier 'jealous' here might give us pause. If the oracle's purpose is to distinguish the innocent from the guilty, then it would be enough to name Leontes a tyrant. Does the extraneous 'jealous' somehow diminish the severity of Leontes's injustice, as if to say that he behaved tyrannically only because of his jealousy or only in matters of love? Or does 'jealous' rather serve to remind us that tyranny is usually greased by venal emotions, such as Macbeth's ambition or Richard III's envy?

Significantly, aside from Apollo, Paulina is the only character to accuse Leontes of tyranny. Announcing the news of Hermione's death, Paulina asks the 'tyrant' what methods of torture he will use to punish her for her harsh words (3.2.172). She condemns his 'tyranny' and again calls him a 'tyrant' (3.2.176, 204). Instead of responding like the typical wrathful tyrant, however, Leontes authorizes Paulina to criticize him freely: 'Thou didst speak but well

/ When most the truth' (3.2.229-30). What do you make of Leontes's swerve away from absolutism at this moment? Has Paulina judged him too harshly? Has Leontes finally learned to adopt the role of (in King James's terms) the 'good king' who expresses 'good will' towards his subjects and heeds the advice of his counsellors?

When the play returns to Sicily sixteen years later, we discover that Leontes has evidently developed an abiding trust in Paulina. Unlike those critics who consider Paulina manipulative and cruel, Laurie Shannon argues that Paulina, motivated by 'goodwill', has 'take[n] up Leontes as a ward to be tutored' and has continued to serve as 'royal physician and counselor of state' (212-13). Patricia Akhimie describes Paulina as an 'unconventional form of ambassador' who practices a 'slow' and 'deliberate' diplomacy as 'an aid to peacemaking' (139-40). In the Writing Matters section below, you will have an opportunity to explore Leontes's transformation from a tyrannical monarch to a monarch who seeks his counsellors' advice. For now, we will conclude our discussion of the political language of *The Winter's Tale* by looking at the dispute between Paulina and Leontes's other counsellors in 5.1. For the first time in the play, Shakespeare depicts courtiers disagreeing with each other about how best to advise their king. Previously, Camillo, Antigonus, Paulina and several Lords had been united in their efforts to disabuse the king of his jealous fantasies. Now Paulina, on the one side, and Cleomenes and Dion, on the other, offer Leontes contrary advice about remarrying. Their debate raises pointed issues about the monarch's responsibility for the continuity of succession.

Although the scene begins by reminding us of the sixteen-year penance that Leontes has undertaken, what is at stake is not just Leontes's spiritual health but the future health of the nation. Leontes cannot forget how his cruelty to his family has made his kingdom '[h]eirless' (5.1.10). Original audience members of *The Winter's Tale* might have connected Hermione with the historical Queen Elizabeth, another queen who died without a biological heir. Cultivating the image of a powerful, independent Virgin Queen, Elizabeth never married, despite the urging of Parliament, the hopes of her male favourites and the courtship of foreign princes. When it became clear that Elizabeth would never bear children, arrangements had to be made to ensure a smooth succession. James VI of Scotland, Elizabeth's cousin, the ruler of a neighbouring kingdom, and a man with a wife and (male) children, was regarded as the best choice to succeed Elizabeth. The question of royal succession, which had been extremely urgent just a decade earlier, would likely have raised strong feelings – or, at the least, vivid memories – for the play's original English audiences.

Paulina, Cleomenes and Dion all express strong feelings about the king's remarriage. When Leontes acknowledges his lack of an heir, Paulina laments the loss of 'she you killed' (5.1.15). Berating Paulina for this bitter remark, Cleomenes advises her to speak in a way that will do 'the time more benefit' (5.1.22). What does it mean to speak in a way that benefits the time? Leontes had earlier accused Camillo of being a 'hovering temporizer, that / Canst with thine eyes at once see good and evil, / Inclining to them both' (1.2.300-2). A 'temporizer' (from the Latin for 'time': *tempus/tempor-*) is a courtier who delivers his counsel not from a considered judgment of 'good and evil', but from a cynical calculation of what will please in the current political climate. Hence 'temporizer' could be considered another name for 'flatterer'. Cleomenes is advising Paulina not to flatter the king, but rather to conform her counsel to the urgent needs of the current political moment. For Cleomenes, honouring Hermione's memory is less important than convincing Leontes to remarry and beget an heir. If Paulina insists on keeping the memory of Hermione alive, Dion insists on the 'remembrance' of the king's 'sovereign name', as if Leontes's royal status has been forgotten during his sixteen-year penance (5.1.25-6). Whereas Paulina asks Leontes to look to the past, to 'her that's gone', Cleomenes and Dion advocate the 'present comfort' of finding a new queen to avoid the dangers of an uncertain succession and to secure the kingdom's 'future good' (5.1.32, 35). How would you characterize the ethical, political and psychological implications of the antithetical advice offered by Leontes's counsellors?

Exercising her authority as chief counsellor, Paulina ends the dispute by instructing Leontes not to worry about the future. Possibly turning to address Leontes directly – editor John Pitcher adds a stage direction, [*to Leontes*], that doesn't appear in the First Folio – Paulina reassures him:

> [*to Leontes*] Care not for issue;
> The crown will find an heir. Great Alexander
> Left his to th'worthiest, so his successor
> Was like to be the best.
>
> (5.1.46-9)

As he was dying, the famous warrior Alexander the Great directed his followers to choose the worthiest among them to succeed him as emperor (Pitcher 47-8n.). Arguably, similar reasoning was responsible for selecting James VI of Scotland to succeed the childless Queen Elizabeth as the English monarch. Paulina's advice has more radical implications, however, than the choice of James to succeed his cousin Elizabeth. In her example, the 'worthiest' successor is not necessarily biologically related to the current monarch, and possibly not even of royal blood. Moreover, in implying that the worth of a successor should be judged not by dynastic lineage but by ability, Paulina hints that biological heirs are not always 'the best' rulers: a dangerous idea in a hereditary monarchy such as Sicily (or Shakespeare's England). In short, Paulina advises that Leontes need not remarry and conceive an heir because an able ruler of the kingdom will be found one way or another. Considering how brutally Leontes had dismissed Paulina's counsel earlier in the play, it is striking how readily he submits to her judgement.

Festive pleasures, festive dangers

With the shift from Sicily in Acts 1-3 to Bohemia in Act 4, *The Winter's Tale* moves from tragic courtly intrigues to comedic country pleasures. Correspondingly, the political language of the early acts is replaced by language centred on 'great creating Nature' (4.4.88) – including 'flowers', 'sheep', 'flock', 'spring', 'summer', 'winds', 'bank' and 'greensward' – and on festive activities such as dressing up, disguising, wooing, eating, drinking, singing, dancing and shopping. The more humble social milieu of the Bohemian sheep-shearing festival facilitates a more relaxed perspective on female sexuality than in Leontes's court. Whereas Leontes resents Hermione's affectionate 'entertainment' of Polixenes, the old Shepherd fondly remembers how his late wife 'welcomed all' guests to her table, serving food at 'his shoulder and his', while Florizel encourages Perdita to be 'sprightly' (energetic) and mirthful when 'entertain[ing]' her guests (1.2.111; 4.4.53, 57, 60). Perdita openly expresses desire for Florizel. At the same time, she repeatedly expresses disdain for theatrical play and forms of artifice, including dressing above or below one's social station, singing scurrilous words in ballads, wearing cosmetics to attract men and even planting hybridized flowers. Looking closely at Perdita's language in 4.4, we will consider what her resistance to artifice might reveal about gender and status hierarchies in Shakespeare's play and culture. In short, we will ask why Florizel seems to enjoy the inversions and transgressions of the sheep-shearing festival so much more than Perdita.

Although it supposedly takes place in ancient, pagan, Bohemia, the sheep-shearing festival recognizably depicts the agricultural, commercial and celebratory customs of rural, Christian, sixteenth-century England (Bristol 163-5; Lupton, *Afterlives* 200-1). Large-scale sheep-shearing such as that organized by the Old Shepherd required 'extensive social cooperation' and a 'very complex division of labor' (Bristol 164). As we saw in the Introduction, Shakespeare created Autolycus out of the 'racy realism of urban satire' (Laroque 8); nonetheless, Autolycus's begging and peddling recall 'the ways that the laboring poor' in rural England 'made ends meet' (Ingram 66). Perdita's anachronistic reference to 'Whitsun pastorals' evokes the English religious/seasonal celebrations at which beggars and peddlers might be found (4.4.134). Whitsun (the seventh Sunday after Easter) marked the commencement of springtime festivities, such as morris dancing, Robin Hood plays and May games. According to François Laroque, such celebrations had 'all gone into an irredeemable decline' by the time of *The Winter's Tale* (1). Thus, he argues, the presence of the cynical, commercializing, Autolycus indicates that Shakespeare is critiquing a naively idealized 'nostalgia for Elizabethan popular culture and rural pastimes' (5). In other words, for Laroque the sheep-shearing scenes provide critical distance on 'comic and popular energies', in part through Perdita's discomfort with festival pleasures (12). Perdita's ambivalence has something to do with her paradoxical status: while actually a princess, she believes herself to be a humble shepherdess; even as a shepherdess, however, she seems majestic, as the language of the scene continually reminds us: her 'acts' are 'queens', she plays a festival 'queen', she seems the 'queen of curds and cream' and, when threatened by the king, she will 'queen it no inch farther' (4.4.5, 146, 161, 454).

Reflecting the idea that Perdita 'smacks of something greater than herself', Florizel describes the sheep-shearing festival as an ordinary event to which Perdita's presence imparts, in the words of Time, an extraordinary 'grace' (4.4.158, 4.1.24). Perdita's 'unusual' festival clothes 'give a life' to 'each part' of her (4.4.1-2). In these, his first words of the play, Florizel speaks in a way that seems simple but evades clear paraphrase. Does 'give a life to' mean 'give birth to', 'resurrect from the dead', or 'animate a lifeless object'? Does 'part' refer to the body parts covered by or framed by clothing (face, arms, torso etc.) or to less embodied personal qualities? Whatever Florizel's words precisely mean, they attribute an ennobling power to Perdita's elegant clothes: she becomes 'Flora', the ancient Roman goddess of flowers; the festival becomes a 'meeting of the petty gods', with Perdita reigning as its 'queen' (2, 4-5). Perhaps Florizel intuitively recognizes in Perdita the princess we know her to be. In any case, the idea that theatrical play has an uncanny transformative power carries throughout the scene.

Disguised as a shepherd to conceal his identity, Florizel takes pleasure in the inversion of everyday roles that humbles his appearance and elevates Perdita's. When Perdita worries about their social transgression, Florizel explains how the gods Jupiter and Neptune, '[h]umbling their deities to love', took the form of 'beasts' in order to get sexual access to mortal women (26-7). Implying that only love could produce such a radical 'transform[ation]', Florizel presents his transformation from prince to shepherd as evidence of his inner 'faith' to Perdita (31, 35). From Florizel's perspective, if his humble appearance proves not his social impropriety but his sincere affection, then Perdita should be happy, not anxious: 'Apprehend / Nothing but jollity'; 'darken not / The mirth o'th'feast'; 'Be merry'; 'Lift up your countenance'; 'let's be red with mirth' (24-5, 41-2, 46, 49, 54).

Whereas Florizel clearly enjoys – or at the least makes an excellent pretence of enjoying – festive play, Perdita continues to express reservations about adopting false roles and appearances. These negative feelings derive from her apparent anxiety about transgressing social, gender and sexual boundaries. In her first speech, Perdita complains to Florizel:

> Your high self,
> The gracious mark o'th'land, you have obscured
> With a swain's wearing, and me, poor lowly maid,
> Most goddess-like pranked up. But that our feasts
> In every mess have folly, and the feeders
> Digest it with a custom, I should blush

> To see you so attired; swoon, I think,
> To show myself a glass.
>
> (7-14)

Through antithesis ('high self' / 'lowly maid'; 'obscured' / 'pranked up'), Perdita suggests that their socially inappropriate apparel has inverted traditional hierarchies of status. Florizel, the heir to the throne, is unrecognizable in the clothing of a 'swain' or peasant; conversely, the socially insignificant Perdita shines like a 'goddess'. To 'prank up' is to 'dress or deck in a smart, bright, or ostentatious manner' (*OED* prank *v*.4, 1.a). Since vanity was a fault conventionally associated with women, female ostentation could always be attributed to sinful pride or even sexual promiscuity. For instance, in *The Excellency of Good Women* (1613), Barnabe Riche writes:

> There be a number of women in these days that of my conscience are both good and honest, and I am sure that they themselves are desirous so to be accounted, and yet if we should judge of them by their outward show, as they use to prank up themselves in their light and gaudy attire, we should judge them to be more courtesan-like than ever was Lais of Corinth or Flora of Rome.
>
> (sig. B2r)

When 'prank[ed] up' in 'light and gaudy attire', even 'good and honest' women might be regarded as courtesans, meaning wealthy, cultivated prostitutes (and note here that Rich associates Flora – whom Perdita is said to resemble in her finery – with sexual promiscuity). Although Perdita does not worry about being read as a courtesan, in the above passage she does express strong reservations about how her appearance, and Florizel's, will be received. Following a strong medial caesura and the turn-word 'but' (line 10), she introduces an analogy between holiday costuming and feasting, activities in which 'folly' (foolishness or playfulness) is customary. If not for such allowed folly, Perdita would 'blush' or 'swoon' to see the sartorial transformations she and Florizel have undergone. Although she might not actually blush or swoon here, what kind of emotions would you say that Perdita is feeling at this moment?

The socially disruptive effects of dressing like someone else, either in the clothes traditionally worn by the opposite sex or in

the fine apparel reserved for the elite, also concerned critics of
the London theatre. These 'anti-theatrical' critics objected to boy
actors wearing women's clothes and imitating women's gestures,
as well as to common actors wearing the attire and adopting the
stately carriage of nobles and monarchs. Stephen Gosson affirms
that 'for a mean person to take upon him the title of a prince, with
counterfeit port and train' constitutes a 'lie'; Anthony Munday
laments that boy actors are 'trained up in filthy speeches, unnatural
and unseemly gestures' (qtd. Pollard 102, 79). According to some
anti-theatricalists, cross-gender or cross-class dressing was not
simply indecent, immoral or subversive, but could actually have
more permanent transformative effects on minds and bodies. Laura
Levine argues that 'at the root of pamphlet attacks' on boy actors
playing female roles lay the fear that costume could actually 'alter
the gender of the male body beneath the costume' (3). Levine cites
Gosson, who claimed that theatre 'effeminates' the mind, and
Philip Stubbes, who complained that wearing women's clothing
could 'adulterate' male gender (qtd. Levine 3-4). Moreover, not
only actors but also spectators could be contaminated by the filthy
stories enacted on stage: 'in the representation of whoredom, all
the people in mind play the whores' (Munday, qtd Pollard 66).

Perdita alludes to these anti-theatrical beliefs when she remarks
that playing the festival queen has changed her 'disposition',
meaning the 'natural tendency or bent of the mind', especially 'in
relation to moral or social qualities' (*OED* disposition, *n.* 6):

> Methinks I play as I have seen them do
> In Whitsun pastorals; sure this robe of mine
> Does change my disposition.
>
> (4.4.133-5)

Although Perdita has observed others ('them') play in 'Whitsun
pastorals', she is distressed about her own participation in a similar
kind of theatrical performance. Editor John Pitcher suggests that
Perdita's admission of a 'change of disposition' refers to her unfamiliar
feelings of 'superior[ity]' as a result of dressing and behaving like a
queen (135n). Although this reading is possible, Perdita's concern
about her changed disposition might also be prompted by an unusual
sexual freedom. She has just expressed the desire for springtime
flowers to strew over Florizel's body 'like a bank for love to lie

and play on' (130): the image is of lovers enjoying erotic dalliance ('play') while reclining on a bank of flowers. In short, Perdita seems to associate acting in a play with sexual play. Playing the false roles of Flora or festival queen, then, might alter Perdita's natural 'disposition' not only from humility to superiority, but from sexual modesty to wantonness, just as the anti-theatrical critics complained occurred in the theatre.

Perdita's objection to planting certain kinds of flowers in her garden, oddly enough, reiterates this association between artifice and sexual transgression. Perdita explains that her garden does not contain carnations or streaked gillyvors, flowers known as 'Nature's bastards' because there 'is an art which in their piedness shares / With great creating Nature' (83, 87-8). Bastards are children whose parents are unmarried; to Leontes, Perdita, born from an adulterous affair, is a 'bastard' (2.3.72). By analogy, gillyvors are 'Nature's bastards' because they are created through the indirect process of cross-fertilization, from which they receive their distinctive 'piedness', or multicoloured streaks. Perdita favours the purity of Nature's creative power over the human 'art' or artifice that can produce hybrid forms. Although Polixenes defends cross-fertilization and grafting by arguing that these arts are not antithetical to but rather made possible by Nature, Perdita still refuses to plant gillyvors, 'No more than, were I painted, I should wish / This youth to say 'twere well, and only therefore / Desire to breed by me' (4.4.101-3). Perdita resolves this debate about the relative merits of nature and art by appealing to sexual morality. She is not 'painted' (does not cover her skin with cosmetics) because artificially enhanced beauty is sexually enticing, producing in men the 'desire to breed'.

The association between face-painting and sexual transgression was familiar to Shakespeare's contemporaries. In the *Anatomy of Abuses* (1583), Philip Stubbes rails against cosmetics:

> S. [St.] *Ciprian* amongst all the rest, saith, a woman through painting and dying of her face showeth herself to be more then whorish. For (saith he) she hath corrupted and defaced (like a filthy strumpet or brothel) the workmanship of God in her. What is this else, but to turn truth into falsehood, with painting and sibbersauces.... S. *Ambrose* saith that from the coloring of faces spring the enticements to vices, and that they which color their

faces do purchase to themselves the blot and stain of chastity. For what a dotage is it (saith he) to change thy natural face which God hath made thee, for a painted face, which thou hast made thyself?

(sigs. F1r-v)

This attack on cosmetics also resonates with the anti-theatrical argument that '[p]layers are evil because they try to substitute a self of their own contriving for the one given them by God' (Barish, *Antitheatrical* 93). Both cosmetics and acting, then, exchange the 'natural', God-given, self for an artificial, constructed, self. Like Stubbes, Perdita understands the use of cosmetics not as an enhancement of the body, but as an adulteration of nature. However, whereas Stubbes explicitly associates cosmetics with sexual transgression, Perdita avoids words like 'whorish', 'strumpet' or 'brothel'. What might be the significance of Perdita's restraint in condemning the sexual implications of cosmetics? In what other terms might we compare Perdita's views with Stubbes'?

When Polixenes accuses Perdita of having seduced Florizel, he justifies her fear of being deemed sexually wanton because of her intimacy with the prince. What do you make of Polixenes's claim? Looking back at the beginning of 4.4, consider how Florizel and Perdita describe or experience the erotic dynamics of their relationship. Do we know if one of them originally wooed the other or if their attraction was mutual? Is this a relationship in which one partner seems the 'wooer' and the other the 'wooed'? Howsoever you answer these questions, Polixenes blames Perdita for distracting Florizel from his princely duties. Calling Perdita a 'fresh piece / Of excellent witchcraft' – meaning '[p]ower or influence like that of a magician; bewitching or fascinating attraction or charm' (*OED*, witchcraft *n*., 2) – Polixenes associates her with women who achieve illicit powers through allegiance to the devil (4.4.427-8). Although Polixenes has heretofore seemed more rational and kind than Leontes, his angry denunciation of Perdita recalls Leontes's branding of Paulina as a 'mankind witch' (2.3.66):

> if ever henceforth thou
> These rural latches to his entrance open,
> Or hoop his body more with thy embraces,

> I will devise a death as cruel for thee
> As thou art tender to't.
>
> (4.4.442-6)

Apt here is Peter Stallybrass's discussion, addressed above, of the early modern expectation that women should keep their bodies sexually closed and enclosed inside the patriarchal household. According to Polixenes, Perdita has violated these norms of femininity by 'open[ing]' the 'latches' of her rural home to Florizel, intimately 'hoop[ing]' his body with her 'embraces'. The 'social disparity between Perdita and Florizel', remarks Ari Friedlander, evokes 'the common figure of the fallen maid', suggesting that the young lovers might have already had illicit (pre-marital) sex, despite their 'equivocal' claims to chastity (501).

Having abandoned her role as festival queen, Perdita finds that she must again falsify her appearance, this time by wearing a disguise to obscure her identity. Camillo directs her,

> take your sweetheart's hat
> And pluck it o'er your brows, muffle your face,
> Dismantle you and, as you can, disliken
> The truth of your own seeming
>
> (654-7)

To 'pluck' Florizel's hat 'over [her] brows', 'muffle [her] face', and 'dismantle' (take off her elegant mantle or robe) is, Perdita complains, to 'bear a part' in yet another 'play' (659-60). Camillo's instruction to 'disliken / The truth of your own seeming' resonates with Perdita's earlier rejection of artifice as a falsification of nature. Although she is eager to return to her shepherdess's duties as an expression of her true self, Perdita must against mispresent herself, this time as a man. Perdita might concur with Stephen Gosson that to cross-dress is to lie:

> The proof is evident, the consequent is necessary, that in stage plays for a boy to put on the attire, the gesture, the passions of a woman... is by outward signs to show themselves otherwise than they are, and so within the compass of a lie, which by Aristotle's judgment is naught of itself, and to be fled.
>
> (qtd. Pollard, *Theater* 102)

Unlike comedies such as *As You Like It* and *Twelfth Night*, *The Winter's Tale* doesn't explicitly address the phenomenon of boy actors who play women who then cross-dress as boys. Nonetheless, the boy actor(s) who played Perdita in early performances would fall under Gosson's censure for lying, as would Perdita for dressing like a queen or wearing a man's hat to 'disliken' her appearance. For Perdita, theatrical playing is less an outlet for imagination or pleasure than it is a worrisome and even dangerous evasion of the 'truth of [her] own seeming' (4.4.657).

Faith, magic and art: The statue scene

The last act of *The Winter's Tale* contains a notable concentration of theological language, including the terms 'blessed', 'chapel', 'divine', 'grace', 'heavens', 'holy', 'image', 'kneel', 'penitence', 'proselytes', 'redeemed/redeems', 'sacred', 'saintlike', 'sect', 'sin', 'superstition', 'trespass' and 'zeal'. Although the public theatre for which Shakespeare wrote was at its core a 'secular, and secularizing institution', religious ways of 'thinking and feeling' inevitably informed stage plays (Dawson 240-1). Shakespeare opens Act 5 by reminding us that for the past sixteen years Leontes has performed a daily ritual of spiritual penance at the graves of his wife and son. Using recognizably theological terms such as 'trespass' (a synonym for 'sin' in the English Tyndale Bible), Cleomenes argues that Leontes has fully paid his spiritual debt:

> Sir, you have done enough, and have performed
> A saint-like sorrow. No fault could you make
> Which you have not redeemed; indeed, paid down
> More penitence than done trespass. At the last
> Do as the heavens have done, forget your evil,
> With them forgive yourself.
>
> (5.1.1-6)

As Sara Saylor argues, the idea that a sinner could 'pay down' or satisfy their sins through the work of penitence recalls the Catholic sacrament of penance (162). Protestants objected to the Catholic notion of satisfaction through works because 'only Christ's sacrifice could satisfy mankind's debt of sin, and it was sinful to presume that human efforts could so do' (Saylor 158; see also Benkert 35-9; Miller 638-40). Nonetheless, while the Protestant *Homily of Repentance* does stress faith in Christ's sacrifice and in God's infusing grace as the foundation of repentance, it also expounds on 'all the inward and outward things' a sinner should do in order to 'return unto God' (Church of England sig. Nnn7v). According to the *Homily*, weeping and mourning 'contain an outward profession of repentance, which is very needful and necessary, that so we may partly set forth the righteousness of God'; however, 'God hath no pleasure in the outward ceremony: but requireth a contrite and humble heart' (sigs. Nnn7v-8r). Echoing this language, Cleomenes insists that Leontes has 'performed' not only an outward profession of repentance but also a 'saint-like sorrow' that proves his contrition. Therefore, Leontes should 'forget' his past sins and 'forgive' himself, as the gods ('heavens') have already done.

The religious language of 5.1 raises some difficult questions that are explored more fully in the final scene of the play. Has Leontes indeed displayed what the *Homily of Repentance* calls a 'contrite and humble heart'? Have the gods forgiven Leontes, as Cleomenes claims? Cleomenes's emphasis on forgiveness contradicts Paulina's warning to Leontes, following Hermione's death, that 'ten thousand' years of extreme penitence would fail to pay for his sins or 'move the gods' to forgive him (3.2.208, 210). Has Leontes earned forgiveness? Does he deserve forgiveness? Does he deserve redemption? Are some sins, no matter how sincerely repented or regretted, simply unforgivable and irredeemable?

Before addressing religious language more directly, let's consider how the final scene of *The Winter's Tale* braids together strands of discourse from the entire play, including the subjects of this chapter's subtopics: women's speech, sovereign rule and performative artifice. Act Five, Scene Three opens with Leontes praising Paulina for speaking her mind as chief counsellor: 'O grave and good Paulina, the great comfort / That I have had of thee!' (1-2). How would you identify the emotion that Leontes is expressing through the initial 'O' or the alliterative sequence of '*gr*ave', '*g*ood' and '*gr*eat'? Paulina's response is dense with political language:

> What, sovereign sir,
> I did not well, I meant well. All my services
> You have paid home, but that you have vouchsafed

With your crowned brother, and these your contracted
Heirs of your kingdoms, my poor house to visit,
It is a surplus of your grace which never
My life may last to answer.

(2-8)

When you recall how terms such as 'sovereign', 'services', 'crowned', 'heirs', 'kingdoms' and 'grace' are used throughout the play to negotiate political relationships, why do you think Paulina might cite so much political language when inviting Leontes into her gallery? How might her economic language ('pa[ying] home', 'poor', 'surplus') recall the language used to describe the responsibilities of political hosts and guests in 1.1 and 1.2? Paulina expresses gratitude for the gift of the king's 'grace': an 'exceptional favour granted by a person in authority' (*OED*, grace *n.* 3a). The imminent encounter with Hermione's statue will expand the meanings of 'grace' to the aesthetic – the 'feature of something which imparts beauty or evokes admiration' (*OED*, grace *n.* 13b) – and the religious – God's 'benevolence towards humanity, bestowed freely and without regard to merit' (*OED*, grace *n.* 1a).

The court's experience of the grace and mystery of Hermione's statue powerfully intertwines the aesthetic and the religious. In the previous scene, the courtiers had attributed to Giulio Romano, the statue's creator, an almost supernatural ability to imitate nature through artifice. Romano was an actual early-sixteenth-century Italian artist who worked primarily as a painter and architect. If Romano were divinely able to infuse 'breath' into his statues, he would 'beguile Nature of her custom, so perfectly he is her ape' (5.2.96-7). In other words, only Romano's mortality prevents him from stealing the Goddess Nature's job (or 'custom') of generating life. Romano is described here as both Nature's rival (implying art's equality with nature) and Nature's 'ape' or imitator (implying art's subordination to nature). Paulina picks up this language when she tells her guests that in Hermione's statue they will 'see the life as lively mocked as ever / Still sleep mocked death' (5.3.19-20). What is the implication, in Paulina's analogy, of art imitating ('mock[ing]') *life* whereas nature, in the form of sleep, imitates *death*? What do Leontes's questions – 'Would you not deem it breathed, and that those veins / Did verily bear blood?' and 'What fine chisel / Could ever yet cut breath?' (64-5, 78-9) – suggest about the experience of encountering an impossibly natural work of art?

With Romano, Shakespeare also alludes to the tale of Pygmalion the sculptor from Ovid's *Metamorphoses*. Disgusted by the promiscuity of local prostitutes, Pygmalion decides to carve a marble woman more perfect than any woman made by nature. Having fallen in love with his creation, Pygmalion kisses, fondles and dresses it up. One day Pygmalion prays to Venus, goddess of love, to make him a woman like his statue. Understanding the artist's true desires, Venus gives life to the statue. In his poem *The Metamorphosis of Pygmalion's Image* (1598), satirist John Marston renders the artist's affection towards his statue in explicitly sexual terms. Because Leontes expresses a desire to touch and kiss Hermione's statue, some scholars have considered the significance of Shakespeare's allusion to the Pygmalion story: an arguably 'misogynist' and 'pornographic fantasy of animation and compliance' (Enterline 24; Langley 322).

Other scholars have noted Giulio Romano's reputation in sixteenth-century Europe as the creator of a notorious series of pornographic images published as *I Modi* ('the positions'). Why would Shakespeare associate Hermione's return to life with the possibly 'degrading implications' of sexually graphic images (Langely 336)? Do you detect any sexual language or gestures in the statue scene? If so, how might such eroticism sit with the spiritual aspects of the scene? Other critics have argued that Hermione's reappearance in the form of a statue purges her of the 'too hot' sexuality that Leontes had found so disturbing: the threat of active female sexual desire 'has been psychically encased in stone', a 'symbolic form of stasis and control' (Traub 45). Embodied in or as a statue, does Hermione return to Leontes as a pornographic fantasy, as a pure monumental object or as something else?

In his initial response to the statue, Leontes speaks the language of the supernatural that gives the scene its atmosphere of mystery and wonder:

I am ashamed. Does not the stone rebuke me
For being more stone than it? O royal piece!
There's magic in thy majesty, which has
My evils conjured to remembrance, and

From thy admiring daughter took the spirits,
Standing like stone with thee.

(5.3.37-42)

To what does Leontes refer when he attributes to the statue the power to 'rebuke' him (in anger? indignation? sorrow?) for being 'more stone than it'? Leontes apostrophizes the statue as a powerful sorcerer who uses 'magic' to 'conjure' (call up, as evil 'spirits') his past 'evils' or sins. This metaphor is remarkable for several reasons. First, despite describing Hermione's statue as 'royal' and 'majestic', Leontes associates it with the necromantic power of witches or sorcerers, who were considered enemies of the crown in early modern England. Second, the pun on 'spirits' connects the statue's magical powers with its aesthetic and commemorative powers as a work of art, which can induce feelings such as shame or 'admir[ation]': a state of wonder that drains the vital forces (bodily spirits) required for action, figuratively turning the body to stone. Thus the necromancy metaphor extends to Perdita the imagined bodily transformation – being turned to stone – that Leontes experiences in his own encounter with the statue. What is the significance of Leontes's imagining that both Perdita and himself partake of the statue's 'stony' nature?

Developing Leontes's discourse of the supernatural, Perdita refers to specific devotional practices that Shakespeare's audience would have recognized as Catholic:

And do not say 'tis superstition, that
I kneel and then implore her blessing. Lady,
Dear queen, that ended when I but began,
Give me that hand of yours to kiss.

(43-6)

Catholic pilgrims travelled to 'chapel[s]' and shrines to ask a patron saint or the Virgin Mary to answer their prayers, such as miraculously healing the sick (86). According to Catholic theology, praying to painted or carved images of saints was a means of communicating with those saints in heaven, who would hear the prayers and act as intercessors with God. Perdita kneels – or prepares to kneel – to the statue of her mother, whom she addresses as 'Lady' and 'Dear queen', possible allusions to epithets for the

Virgin Mary such as 'Our Lady', 'Blessed Lady', 'Blessed Mother' and 'Queen of Heaven'. Perdita also moves to kiss the statue's hand, an act that Protestant theologians would have certainly regarded as 'superstition': a 'religious belief, ceremony or practice considered to be irrational, unfounded, or based on fear or ignorance' (*OED*, superstition, *n*. 5a). Protestants regarded as superstition those Catholic ceremonies that were not based in the authority of the scriptures and that seemed to foreground the sensual or material over the spiritual, such as kneeling to or kissing lifeless stone statues, which were often described as 'idols'.

Reformers also objected to religious images as material 'similitudes' of the divine, 'representations of that which could not or should not be represented' (O'Connor 368). In *The Theater of the Pope's Monarchy* (1584), for instance, Philip Stubbes – one of the anti-theatrical critics cited above – decries as 'horrible superstition' such Catholic practices, beliefs and objects as 'invocation to saints, transubstantiation, adoration of images,... lady psalters [rosaries], tapers, candles, beads, censings, ringings, perfumings, and legions of like trumperies, which the word of God knoweth not' (sigs. 4r-v). Stubbes uses the same word to describe Catholic devotion – 'trumpery' – that Autolycus uses to describe the cheap trash he hawks (4.4.602). Scholars disagree about whether or not *The Winter's Tale* takes a specific position on Catholic and Protestant beliefs and practices, and, if so, what that position is (see Beckwith; Benkert; Diehl, 'Rebuke' and 'Strike'; Dolan; Hunt, 'Syncretistic'; Jensen; Lupton, *Afterlives*; Lim, 'Knowledge'; Miller; O'Connell; Strier; Vanita; Waldron). So it is reasonable to ask if Perdita's use of 'superstition' would necessarily evoke condemnation of the adoration of images. Is Perdita's reverence towards the statue presented more positively than Stubbes's account of Catholics' reverence towards their objects of devotion? Perdita in fact disavows that her behaviour constitutes 'superstition'. What else might her kneeling to and kissing Hermione's statue signify?

At the climax of 5.3, Paulina appears to produce a 'miracle made possible by faith' (Tiffany 9). Before she animates Hermione's statue, however, Paulina acknowledges that she might be accused of witchcraft (being 'assisted / By wicked powers' [90-1]). Whereas Leontes had figuratively attributed to the statue the necromantic power of conjuring his wicked deeds, Paulina implies her ability literally to perform magic by making a statue move. Nonetheless, she insists that she is not undertaking an 'unlawful business' (96). What are we about to witness: a miracle, a magic trick or an elaborate theatrical illusion? 'It is required / You do awake your faith', Paulina instructs her guests, presumably Leontes chief among them (94-5). 'Faith', like 'grace', is a multivalent keyword of *The Winter's Tale*: it indexes religion ('belief in a god or gods and in the authenticity of divine revelation'); politics ('allegiance owed to a superior'); and love ('faithfulness, fidelity, loyalty') (*OED* faith, *n.* 1.a., 1.b., 5). What kind of 'faith' does Paulina's miraculous/magical/theatrical marvel 'require'? What is the significance of her use of the word 'awake' in speaking of faith? Is Leontes being asked to affirm his belief in Paulina, in the gods, in himself, in Hermione or in something else?

In the Writing Matters section below, you will have an opportunity to analyse the language of the 'spell' that Paulina speaks to 'make the statue move' (105, 98). In the remainder of this chapter, we will focus on how the language of the final scene allows us to interpret the animation of Hermione's statue as a magical, miraculous or theatrical event. To get at these different possibilities, we need to scrutinize what we believe has really happened: did Hermione die of grief from Mamillius's death, or has she lived secretly with Paulina for sixteen years, awaiting Perdita's return? If she died, how has she returned to life sixteen years later? Polixenes delivers essentially the same, unanswered, demand to 'make it manifest where she has lived, / Or how stolen from the dead' (114-15). Until the final scene of the play, all the evidence seems to point to the fact of Hermione's death. At the end of her trial, Hermione swoons and is carried offstage; shortly thereafter, Paulina re-enters to announce Hermione's death. Leontes asks to see 'the dead bodies of my queen and son' and vows to visit the 'chapel where they lie' every day (3.4.232, 236). Having seen Hermione's ghost, Antigonus concludes that she 'hath suffered death' (3.3.41).

If Hermione has truly died, we need to account for her resurrection in the form of a stone statue. Are we to imagine that, perhaps to shield her from mortal grief, Apollo supernaturally 'preserved' Hermione's body in the form of a statue that could be restored to living flesh through Paulina's intermediation (5.3.127)? In this case of suspended animation, the statue would 'present a body or a pose arrested in time, arresting time itself.... the reification of something once living and mutable' (Gross 15). Or has Paulina commissioned an artist to craft an incredibly life-like statue of the former queen (appropriately 'aged' with wrinkles to convey the passage of time), which she has the ability magically to bring to life? Theoretically, there is no good reason to reject these scenarios: countless horror, science fiction and fantasy movies feature magical, biological, technological, supernatural or demonic transformations of bodies into different states of life or death. As a work of imagination, *The Winter's Tale* has no obligation to conform to any standard of the merely possible.

Moreover, classical precedent for such a fantastic transformation can be found not only in the Ovidian tale of Pygmalion, discussed above, but also in the play *Alcestis* (438 BC) by the Greek tragedian Euripides, which Shakespeare might have read in a sixteenth-century Latin translation (Dewar-Watson). In the form of a 'humble swain', as Florizel knows, Apollo helped Admetus to win the princess Alcestis as his wife (4.4.30). Later, to save her husband's life, Alcestis agrees to die in his stead. The hero Heracles rescues Alcestis from the underworld, restoring her to life; however, not yet 'purified' of death, Alcestis remains silent during the rest of *Alcestis*, thus throwing her restoration into question (Burnette 441). Polixenes's questioning if Hermione has been 'stolen from the dead' recalls Heracles's rescue of Alcestis from death's grasp (5.3.115). Can Paulina, like Heracles, restore the dead to life, or, like Venus in the Pygmalion story, animate lifeless matter?

Such a reading raises difficult theological and philosophical questions. If a stone statue of Hermione has come to life, does the mortal body of the woman who died sixteen years earlier still lie in the grave? If so, will or should Leontes continue to mourn at the grave of the wife whose death his actions precipitated? Would a Hermione magically or supernaturally created from stone be the 'same' Hermione who died all those years ago? These questions touch upon the theology of resurrection in early modern Christianity, according to which 'the same flesh that lived, died, and decayed was to rise from the grave' on Judgement Day (Lambert 354). For reformer John Calvin, the doctrine of resurrection showed that 'earthly things were but temporary, and in turn, what appeared utterly lost might be restored' (Lambert 359). Does imagining Hermione's 'lost' body 'restored' as stone-made-flesh offer the same hopeful message that Calvin finds in Christian resurrection?

A more prosaic but no less implausible reading of the play would posit that Hermione arranged with Paulina to fake her death and to live secretly on Paulina's estate until Perdita's return. Presumably, then, Antigonus is visited not by the ghost of Hermione, but rather by a dream vision or, as in the early modern Protestant theory of ghosts, by a devil disguised in human form – although the latter, extremely disturbing, possibility is never explicitly entertained in *The Winter's Tale* as it is in *Hamlet*. Julie Crawford regards the sixteen years that Paulina and Hermione 'have spent together keeping a secret' as the play's 'most memorable emblem of *consilium*' (counsel), which was often gendered female in political allegories (128). Upon Perdita's return, Hermione might have simply revealed that she has been alive all along. Instead, it is reported that Giulio Romano has for 'many years' been fashioning a statue 'in the keeping of Paulina' (5.2.93-4). Hermione and Paulina have evidently arranged for the ruse of Hermione's death to be answered by the ruse of her return to life in the form of a masterfully carved statue. Since the statue *is* actually Hermione, it is no surprise that Paulina's deceived guests marvel at its lifelikeness: it is wrinkled with age, strikes a natural posture, has blood in its veins, and seems to move, breathe and exude warmth.

Although this interpretation of Hermione's return might seem more plausible than the alternative, in which a statue magically comes to life, it also raises some difficult questions. Why would Hermione fake her death and live with Paulina? Does allowing a guilt-ridden Leontes to believe for sixteen years that he has killed his wife constitute a 'long and filthy trick' tantamount to 'torture' (Mallin)? What might the women have hoped to accomplish in devising this elaborate performance of reanimation or resurrection through a statue? As Abbe Blum writes, the 'impulse to monumentalize is, on one level, to remember, conjure up, commemorate what is valuable – often by altering, idealizing, idolizing the original proportions of a notable person, action, event' (99). At the same time, Blum continues, to monumentalize 'often involves the effacement of the object of desire' or the 'projection' of one's own needs and fantasies onto an 'external object' (99). For Paulina's audience, does the 'monumentalizing' of Hermione commemorate, enhance or idealize the late queen's value? Does it 'efface' Hermione, subjecting her to viewers' own needs and fantasies? To ask these questions another way, what effect does this scene have on you as a reader or (imagined) audience member? How is your experience of Hermione in 5.3 informed by your memory of what has occurred in the first part of the play?

The language of the last scene, which alternates between identifying Hermione's statue as 'Hermione' (a person) and as a 'statue' (an object) contributes to the uncertainty over whether the statue is composed of stone or flesh. Referring to 'the statue of her [Perdita's] mother', Leontes separates the art object from the absent woman it represents (5.3.14). Paulina, however, collapses the distinction between object and person through an analogy: 'As she lived peerless, / So her dead likeness I do well believe / Excels whatever yet you looked upon' (14-16). The statue is not only a 'likeness' of Hermione, it is *like* her in being 'peerless': it 'excels' all other art just as Hermione excelled all other people. During this scene, Paulina refers to the statue as 'it' and 'her' as if it were simultaneously, or alternately, both sculpture and woman (17-18, 70, 81, 98). Leontes addresses the 'dear stone' directly, as if it could hear and respond to him in Hermione's voice: 'Chide me, dear stone, that I may say indeed / Thou art Hermione' (24-5). Perdita addresses the statue as 'Lady, / Dear queen', (possibly) kneels to it/her, and asks its/her blessing as well as its/her hand to kiss; having restored Hermione, Paulina instructs Perdita to '[k]neel, / And pray your mother's blessing' (44-5, 119-20). Finally, we might consider whether Paulina's 'spell' is addressed to a statue being magically compelled to come alive, or to a woman pretending to be a statue, or possibly to neither or both. To whom/what is Paulina speaking when she orders, 'be stone no more', 'Come, / I'll fill your grave up' and 'Bequeath to death your numbness' (99-102)?

In the brief moments before the play ends, mysteries linger. The embedded stage directions spoken by Polixenes and Camillo indicate that Hermione 'embraces' Leontes and 'hangs about his neck' (111-12). What might these physical gestures express? What range of emotions (e.g. fear, relief, confusion, joy, wonder, remorse and so on) can you imagine Hermione and Leontes feeling at this moment, and how might actors try to convey these particular emotions? Because of Hermione's initial silence, Paulina's guests express puzzlement at the statue's movement. What do they think is happening? Leontes is unsure '[i]f this be magic' or not; Camillo is unsure '[i]f she pertain to life', that is, if Hermione is really alive (110, 113). Camillo proposes that Hermione speak in order to prove that she lives. Polixenes enjoins Hermione to explain either 'where she has lived' for the past sixteen years, or how she has been 'stolen from the dead' (114-15). Responding to this collective amazement, Paulina concedes that 'it appears' Hermione lives (117). Hermione speaks exclusively to Perdita, blessing her and asking questions about her life; she doesn't say a word to Leontes. What do we make of what Hermione says and does not say? As one critic asks, 'Is the embracing of her jealous husband a sincere sign of Hermione's love and forgiveness? Or is it perhaps merely the *performance* of reconciliation?' (Thomas 91).

How we interpret the brief aftermath of Hermione's restoration will significantly shape our sense of the play's generic status as comedy, tragedy, tragicomedy, romance or something else. Both in scholarship and on stage, interpretations of the final scene of *The Winter's Tale* have shifted from an earlier emphasis on forgiveness and reconciliation to a more recent acknowledgement of the possible obstacles to a harmonious conclusion. Readings or performances that stress the joy of Hermione's reunion with Leontes are responding, in part, to the pressures of genre: the First Folio of Shakespeare's plays, as noted in the Introduction, classifies *The Winter's Tale* as a comedy, and we generally expect comedies to end on a happy note. Even if we were to reclassify *The Winter's Tale* as a tragicomedy or dramatic romance, these genres also are essentially comedic in structure, as they generally end with some form of uplifting reconciliation or restitution. A typical feature of Shakespeare's late romances (*The Tempest*, *Cymbeline*, *Pericles*, and *The Winter's Tale*) is the reunion of long-separated family members, often fathers and daughters. Moreover, recall that Shakespeare significantly lightens the grim ending of his primary source, Greene's *Pandosto*, in which the queen remains dead and the king, wracked with guilt, kills himself. *The Winter's Tale* clearly avoids moving that close to tragedy in its final moments.

Nonetheless, the emergence since the 1970s of New Historicist, Feminist, Marxist and other strains of progressive criticism has made it harder to credit the notion that Shakespeare's endings are simply happy, or happy in any simple way. Drawing attention to social inequalities and structures of power, these critical modes often eschew sentimentalism for a hard-edged analysis of the exclusions, repressions or silences that accompany the illusion of social harmony, which is often cited in more traditional scholarship as the sign of a happy ending. In short, such critics pointedly ask of the happy ending: happy for whom? They are apt to argue that socially dominant institutions traditionally said to provide stability and happiness – marriage, family, law, government – actually work to sustain the power inequalities that benefit those at the top. Scholars who practice these modes of criticism, therefore, would urge scepticism at Paulina's blithe assertion that those in the final scene of *The Winter's Tale* are 'precious winners all' (5.3.132). Who decides what counts as winning? Do some characters win more than others? If some are winners, are others losers?

Writing matters

In this section, you will have the opportunity to explore the languages of female authority, politics, festivity and religion in *The Winter's Tale*. For each of these topics, I provide two or three writing prompts: the first features a primary (early modern) text that addresses an issue relevant in some way to *The Winter's Tale*; the following prompts ask you to focus on the specific words, allusions and figures of speech through which the play addresses these issues.

Women's speech and authority

A. In 1615, Joseph Swetnam published a misogynist screed called *The Arraignment of Lewd, Idle, Froward, and Unconstant Women*. Swetnam's book, which 'gathered together misogynist commonplaces from the debate over women throughout the preceding century in England' provoked three published responses, at least one of which was written by an actual woman (Jones 45). In the excerpt below, Swetnam complains of the bitterness of women's tongues, a topic that resonates with the characterization of Paulina as a woman unafraid to criticize even her king. For this exercise, first paraphrase Swetnam's argument in a few sentences. Then discuss how Swetnam's perspective on female speech illuminates (or fails to illuminate) the character of Paulina, particularly in her conflicts with Leontes. You might wish to consider the following issues in your analysis. How do Swetnam and Shakespeare use the word 'tongue' in relation to women's speech and authority? According to the OpenSourceShakespeare concordance, 'tongue' appears thirteen times in *The Winter's Tale*; after looking up each of these appearances, discuss any of them useful for your argument about Paulina. In her exchanges with Antigonus (2 3), does Paulina resemble the scolding wife portrayed by Swetnam? How are animal metaphors used in both texts to explain women's habits of speech? Even when the author's attitude is explicitly critical, as is certainly the case with Swetnam, do his words allow the possibility of seeing the sharp-tongued woman as an appealing figure?

From Joseph Swetnam, *The Arraignment of... Women* (1615):

There is no woman but either she hath a long tongue, or a longing tooth, and they are two ill neighbors, if they dwell together: for the one will lighten thy purse, if it be still pleased, and the other will waken thee from thy sleep, if it be not charmed. Is it not strange of what kind of metal a woman's tongue is made of, that neither correction can chastise, nor faire means quiet: for there is a kind of venom in it, that neither by fair means nor foul they are to be ruled. All beasts by man are made tame, but a woman's tongue will never be lame; it is but a small thing, and seldom seen, but it is often heard, to the terror and utter confusion of many a man.

Therefore, as a sharp bit curbs a froward horse, even so a curst woman must be roughly used: but if women could hold their tongues, then many times men would hold their hands. As the best mettled blade is mixt with iron, even so the best woman that is, is not free from faults: the goodliest gardens are not free from weeds, no more is the best nor the fairest woman from ill deeds....

Divers beasts, and fowl, by nature have more strength in one part of the body then in another, as the eagle in the beak, the unicorn in the horn, the bull in the head, the bear in his arms, the horse in his breast, the dog in his teeth, the serpent in his tail. But a woman's chief strength is in her tongue. The serpent hath not so much venom in his tail as she hath in her tongue; and as the serpent never leaveth hissing and stinging, and seeking to do mischief: even so, some women are never well, except they be casting out venom with their tongues, to the hurt of their husbands or of their neighbors.

(sigs. F4v-G1r)

B. For this exercise, use techniques of close reading to analyse the significance of the way that Leontes and Paulina speak to each other in 5.1, particularly in contrast to their interaction in 2.3. You might consider the following questions in formulating your argument. What words does Leontes use when addressing Paulina in 5.1? How would you describe their relationship in that scene? How do Leontes's views concerning women's speech and authority seem to have changed since 2.3? What is the significance of Cleomenes's interruptions (5.1.20-3, 73, 75)? What is the significance of the brief exchange between Leontes and Paulina at the end of the scene (222-7)?

Obedience and resistance

A. In this exercise, you will consider Paulina's charges of tyranny against Leontes (3.2.172, 204) in the context of the account of tyrants and absolute kings written by one of Shakespeare's contemporaries, Sir Thomas Smith. In his book about the English government, *De Republica Anglorum* (1583), Smith distinguishes the just king, who 'doth administer the commonwealth by the laws of the same and by equity, and doth seek the profit of the people as much as his own', from the tyrant or absolute monarch, who exercises unlimited power (sig. B3v). For this assignment, first paraphrase Smith's argument in a paragraph. Then, using evidence from the play, explain whether or not Leontes conforms to Smith's definition of the tyrant/absolute king. Note that when Smith refers to the 'wealth' of the people, he means 'weal' – a general ideal of the political health of the nation, as in the term 'commonweal'. You might wish to address some of the following issues in your argument. Does Leontes use his power in the way that the tyrant/absolute king does, according to Smith? Does he commit what Smith calls 'horrible' acts? Does Leontes care about the welfare of his kingdom and subjects? Does he display any respect for the gods, what is right or the law, as Smith claims a good king does?

From Sir Thomas Smith, *De Republica Anglorum* (1583):

A tyrant they name him, who by force cometh to the monarchy against the will of the people, breaketh laws already made at his pleasure, maketh other without the advice and consent of the

people, and regardeth not the wealth of his commons but the
advancement of himself, his faction, and kindred .... (sig. B3v)

But as such absolute administration in time of war when all
is in arms, and when laws hold their peace because they cannot
be heard, is most necessary: so in time of peace, the same is very
dangerous, as well to him that doth use it, and much more to the
people upon whom it is used. Whereof the cause is the frailty of
man's nature, which (as Plato saith) cannot abide or bear long
that absolute and uncontrolled authority, without swelling into
too much pride and insolency. And therefore the Romans did
wisely, who would not suffer any man to keep the Dictatorship
above five months, because the Dictators (for that time) had this
absolute power, which some Greeks named a lawful tyranny....
And this kind of [absolute] rule among the Greeks is called
τύρανις [tyranis], which of itself at the first was not a name
odious. But because they who had such rule, at the first, did for
the most part abuse the same, waxed insolent and proud, unjust,
and not regarding the commonwealth, committed such acts as
were horrible and odious, as killing men without cause, abusing
their wives and daughters, taking and spoiling all men's goods
at their pleasures, and were not shepherds as they ought to be,
but rather robbers and devourers of the people; whereof some
were contemners of God, as Dionysius, other while they lived
like devils, and would yet be adored and accompted for Gods, as
Caius Caligula and Domitian. That kind of administration and
manner also, at the first not evil, hath taken the signification and
definition of the vice of the abusers, so that now both in Greek,
Latin, and English a tyrant is counted he who is an evil king, and
who hath no regard to the wealth of his people, but seeketh only
to magnify himself and his, and to satisfy his vicious and cruel
appetite, without respect of God, of right or of the law: because
that for the most part they who have had that absolute power
have been such. (sigs. B4r-C1r)

B. Earlier in this chapter, we explored the importance of political
counsel in *The Winter's Tale*. Camillo, Antigonus and Paulina all
counsel Leontes to reverse his vengeful course of action. For this
exercise, use techniques of close reading to analyse the political
language of the anonymous Lord's speech (2.3.145-51, beginning
'Beseech your highness, give us better credit'), paying particular

attention to the rhetorical strategies he uses to persuade Leontes. You might consider addressing the following issues. What is the significance of the language the Lord uses to address Leontes? How does the Lord seem to understand the proper relationship between counsellor and king? Does the Lord use any keywords of political discourse found elsewhere in *The Winter's Tale*? (Use a concordance to look up any possible keywords from the passage and to identify how they are used throughout the play). Consider the possible effects of any poetic and rhetorical devices you find in the passage, e.g. caesurae, end-stopped or enjambed lines, sentence length, metrical variation, puns etc.

Festive pleasures, festive dangers

A. Our discussion of the sheep-shearing festival addressed Perdita's concerns about socially inappropriate clothing. In his satire *The Anatomy of Abuses* (1583), Philip Stubbes rails against the abuses of apparel in sixteenth-century England. For this exercise, first paraphrase Stubbes's argument in a paragraph. Next, using evidence from *The Winter's Tale*, explain to what degree Perdita's views on fancy clothing align with Stubbes's. On which points might Perdita agree or disagree with Stubbes? Does Perdita share Stubbes's evaluation of the difference between the 'natural' and the 'artificial'? According to Perdita and to Stubbes, who or what is responsible for ostentatious apparel?

> From Philip Stubbes, *The Anatomy of Abuses* (1583):
>
> [God clothed Adam and Eve in leather because] he would [that] this their mean and base attire should be as a rule, or pedagogy unto us, to teach us [that] we ought rather to walk meanly and simply, than gorgeously or pompously: rather serving present necessity than regarding the wanton appetites of our lascivious minds.... his blessed will is, that we should rather go an ace beneath our degree, than a jot above.... And if the Lord would not, that the attire of Adam should have been a sign or pattern of mediocrity unto us, he both in mercy would and in his almighty power could have invested them in silks, velvets, satins, grosgrains, gold, silver, and what not. But the Lord our God foresaw that if he had clothed man in rich and gorgeous attire

(such is our proclivity to sin) he would have been proud thereof, as we see it is come to pass at this day (God amend it) and thereby purchase to himself, his body, and soul, eternal damnation (sigs. C5r-v).... So that when they have all these goodly robes upon them, women seem to be the smallest part of themselves, not natural women but artificial women, not women of flesh and blood, but rather puppets or mammets [idols] of rags and clouts compact together. So far hath this canker of pride eaten into the body of the commonwealth that every poor yeoman's daughter, every husbandman's daughter, and every cottager's daughter will not spare to flaunt it out, in such gowns, petticoats, and kirtles, as these... whereby it cometh to passe, that one can scarcely know who is a noble woman, who is an honorable, or worshipful woman from them of the meaner sort....

(sigs. F6v-F7r)

B. This exercise gives you the chance to explore how mythological allusions might illuminate issues of gender, desire and play in the sheep-shearing scene. Expressing his affection for Perdita, Florizel compares her to Flora and himself to Jupiter, Neptune and Apollo (4.4.2, 27-31). As she distributes flowers to her guests, Perdita recalls the myth of Proserpina (116-18). Perhaps surprisingly, four of these five classical allusions involve rape. Raped by Zephyrus, god of the west wind, the nymph Chloris was transformed into Flora, the Roman goddess of flowers and springtime. Jupiter appeared to the princess Europa in the form of a white bull and carried her away to the island of Crete, where he raped her. Neptune carried the maiden Theophane to the island of Crumissa, turned himself into a ram and her into a ewe to obscure their identities and then raped her. Finally, Prosperina, daughter of the goddess Ceres, was gathering flowers one day when Dis (or Pluto), god of the underworld, abducted her, took her to his kingdom, raped her and made her his wife. For this exercise, use evidence from the play to formulate an argument about the possible significance of these allusions to rape. You might wish to consider the following questions. How does Florizel use these myths as part of an argument he is making to Perdita? What is the significance of Perdita's recollection of Proserpina? How do these allusions affect your understanding of the relationship between Florizel and Perdita, if at all? Might these allusions have anything to do with Florizel's and Perdita's divergent attitudes about play and disguise?

Faith, magic and art: The statue scene

A. Above we examined the religious language of the play's final scene, particularly as it attributes a majestic power to Hermione's statue. In the anti-Papal polemic *The Rocks of Christian Shipwrack* (1618), Marco Antonio de Dominis, the Archbishop of Spalato (Croatia), condemns the Catholic practice of praying to statues as idolatry: the blasphemous worshipping of man-made objects. For this exercise, first write a paragraph in which you present de Dominis's argument in your own words. Next, develop an argument about whether or not the statue scene in *The Winter's Tale* depicts the kind of idolatry that de Dominis condemns. You might wish to consider some of the following questions when formulating your argument. According to de Dominis, what was the origin of worshipping images? Do Leontes and Perdita behave towards Hermione's statue the way that Catholics, according to de Dominis, behave towards statues of the Virgin Mary? To what degree does Paulina's chapel resemble the elaborately decorated chapels described by de Dominis? Might Hermione's statue resemble not a statue of a saint, but rather a tomb effigy (a sculpture of the deceased) in a church (Belsey, *Eden* 108-20)? Does Paulina's management of Leontes and Perdita in their encounter with Hermione's statue in any way resemble 'Churchmen's' management of Catholic believers in de Dominis's account? Ultimately, can you draw any conclusions from this exercise about what constitutes an effective or accurate use of historical documents in the analysis of a literary text?

> From Bishop Marco Antonio de Dominis, *The Rocks of Christian Shipwrack* (1618):
>
> But after that [ancient times] the covetousness of men did run on, inventing and forging of miracles to draw on the people's devotion towards some *Image*, and so their contributions under pretense of lamps, ornaments, and other material embellishments. Thence began they to teach, that there was a certain proper religious worship due to the *Image* itself, and then my idle ministers began to light lamps to them, to burn incense to them, to adore them, to kneel down and make their prayers before them. Hence arose that abuse, that none under the Papacy [Catholicism] knoweth

how to pray without he have before him some petty statue or picture, either painted or printed, especially of the crucifix, and of our Lady. And the churchmen do willfully infuse true and proper idolatry into the minds of the ignorant common people, whilst they erect stately churches, curious chapels, with so many enclosures, vestries, curtains, lamps, torches, indulgences; whilst they carry them in procession with such furniture and outward pomp, being an external religious worship, which pertaineth unto God. They command and compel every man to fall down on his knees and adore them, whereupon the silly people conceiveth a certain divinity to be in them, and without any reflection at all *ad prototypum* – to the principal copy – they offer their vows and their prayers to that stock or stone, to this cloth or tablet, and expect immediately from that very *Image* the grace which they request, even of eternal life. It is not to be doubted, but that the more part of the vulgar commits most proper and formal idolatry with some *Images*. And the doctrine, which some learned Papists [Catholics] do teach, namely, that unto *Images,* as *Images,* a proper religious worship is due, must of necessity make even the wise and learned amongst them to idolatrize formally.

(149-50)

B. This exercise will give you the opportunity to explore the language of the 'spell' that Paulina uses to animate Hermione's statue (5.3.98-109). A spell is a 'set of words, a formula or verse, supposed to possess occult or magical powers; a charm or incantation; a means of accomplishing enchantment or exorcism' (*OED*, spell *n.1*, 3.a.). When considering the definition of spell as incantation, it's useful to know that the etymology of 'incantation' comes from Latin *incantare, in-* + *cantare*: to sing or chant (*OED*, incant, *v.*). Referring both to the *OED* definition and to the witches' spell in *Macbeth* (4.1.4-38), analyse the significance of the language of Paulina's spell in terms of its powers, motives and/or effects. Some questions you might wish to consider: does anything in Paulina's speech resemble a magic 'formula' or 'incantation'? Does Paulina use any words that might seem to possess 'occult or magical powers'? Paulina insists that her spell is 'lawful', unlike, presumably, the kind of spell used by the Witches in *Macbeth* (*WT* 5.3.104). Comparing Paulina's language to that of the Witches, how could you help her prove her claim of lawfulness? How would you describe the effects that Paulina's spell produces on the statue as well as on those present in the chapel?

FIRST WITCH
  Round about the cauldron go,
    In the poisoned entrails throw.
  Toad that under cold stone
  Days and nights has thirty-one,
  Sweltered venom sleeping got[1],
  Boil thou first i'th'charmèd pot.
ALL
  Double, double, toil and trouble,
  Fire burn, and cauldron bubble.
SECOND WITCH
  Fillet of a fenny snake[2],
  In the cauldron boil and bake.
  Eye of newt and toe of frog,
  Wool of bat and tongue of dog,
  Adder's fork[3] and blind-worm's sting,
  Lizard's leg and owlet's wing,
  For a charm of powerful trouble,
  Like a hell-broth boil and bubble.
ALL
  Double, double, toil and trouble,
  Fire burn, and cauldron bubble.
THIRD WITCH
  Scale of dragon, tooth of wolf,
  Witches' mummy, maw and gulf[4]
  Of the ravined[5] salt-sea shark,
  Root of hemlock digged i'th'dark,
  Liver of blaspheming Jew,
  Gall of goat, and slips of yew
  Slivered[6] in the moon's eclipse,
  Nose of Turk, and Tartar's lips,
  Finger of birth-strangled babe

---

[1] for 31 days, the toad has produced venom during sleep
[2] slice of a swamp snake
[3] serpent's forked tongue
[4] mummified flesh, stomach and gullet
[5] ravenous
[6] cut off

> Ditch-delivered by a drab[1],
> Make the gruel thick and slab[2].
> And thereto add a tiger's chaudron[3]
> For th'ingredience of our cauldron.
> ALL
> Double, double, toil and trouble,
> Fire burn, and cauldron bubble.
> SECOND WITCH Cool it with a baboon's blood,
> Then the charm is firm and good.

C. This exercise gives you a chance to explore in depth the conclusion of *The Winter's Tale*, particularly in terms of the generic expectations that we addressed in the Introduction. Using evidence primarily from the last forty or so lines of the play, explain where you think things stand as *The Winter's Tale* comes to a close. You might address some of the following questions. Is the mood at the end of the play joyful, melancholy or something else? How satisfying or disappointing is the ending? What questions remain unanswered, and what is the significance of those silences? How do particular characters fare? Are we given any hint of what life might now be like for Leontes, Hermione, Paulina, Perdita or Polixenes? Does Hermione forgive Leontes? Is it possible to forgive someone without verbalizing that forgiveness (Lupton, 'Forgiveness' 649)? Has Leontes changed? What has he learned? What do you make of Paulina's claim that those present are 'precious winners all' (5.3.131)? Why, in her last words, does Paulina attribute 'exultation' to the others and '[l]amentation' to herself (133, 137)? In his response to Paulina – the final speech of the play – does Leontes say anything about happiness? What do you make of Leontes's proposal that Paulina marry Camillo? What is the significance of the fact that neither Paulina nor Camillo verbally responds to this proposal? What does Leontes's final speech seem intended to accomplish? What does it accomplish, in your interpretation?

---

[1] whore
[2] viscous
[3] entrails

4

Writing and language skills

In the previous four chapters, you have had opportunities to try out many different writing, research and interpretive skills: paraphrasing; looking up words in a concordance and in the *OED*; translating language into visual imagery; identifying how editors modernize original editions of Shakespeare's plays; analysing rhetorical figures in verse and prose; distinguishing among forms of speech such as soliloquy, oration and report; and reading Shakespeare in historical context. Building on Writing Matters units from previous chapters, this chapter will provide suggestions for identifying essay topics – including both 'traditional' and 'creative' approaches – and strengthening your analytical writing. I will also offer guidance in composing the various parts of a critical essay.

Choosing an essay topic I

One of the most challenging tasks is identifying an essay topic. Fortunately, there are many ways to go about selecting a topic. All of them have something in common: they help you to identify the passages, topics or questions that you feel motivated to explore in more depth. It's much easier to write a successful essay when you focus on an issue for which you can muster up some genuine curiosity and enthusiasm. When presenting possible topics below, I always provide a series of questions, because asking questions is an excellent way to begin shaping a thesis for your essay. Often, a thesis statement serves as your answer to a question of interpretation – not a question of fact – that different readers might properly answer in different ways. The primary task of your essay is to persuade your readers of the value, significance and plausibility of your answer.

You might consider several 'pre-writing' activities to help you with the 'invention' stage of your essay, which comprises choosing a topic, shaping that topic, and formulating and organizing your ideas before you begin drafting your essay. Pre-writing strategies include brainstorming, clustering or mapping, freewriting, listing, outlining and so on. A good general discussion of invention strategies, available for free on-line, is Michelle Trim's and Megan Lynn Isaac's 'Reinventing Invention: Discovery and Investment in Writing'. Below, I offer some options for identifying topics for an essay on *The Winter's Tale* based on the reading, research and writing skills you have already practised in this book.

Re-reading the reading journal

If you have been keeping a reading journal, you probably already have much more material than you can use for a single essay. Re-reading your annotations and analyses, identify any passages from the play that continue to spark your interest or raise compelling questions. These might be passages that you would like to understand more completely, that strike you as central to character or plot development, or that simply impress you with their use of language, imagery or rhetorical figures. For instance, let's say that in your journal you had transcribed and annotated the speeches in which Polixenes threatens Perdita (4.4.427-31, 439-46). In the commentary for your annotation, you had noted the parallel between Polixenes's rage at Perdita and Leontes's rage at Hermione earlier in the play. This parallel raises many questions that could be further explored in an essay. For instance, what is the significance of the reappearance of a raging patriarch in the more comedic, pastoral world of the sheep-shearing festival? What are we to make of the fact that not only Leontes but also Polixenes desires to punish a woman for her (supposed) sexual transgressions? Along with any similarities you note, how do these two situations differ? Do Leontes and Polixenes express their anger in the same terms? How might you compare the causes, motives and consequences of Leontes's and Polixenes's anger? A strong thesis might be formulated as the answer to one (or more) of these questions.

Attending to the plot

You might have been intrigued by the workings of the plot of *The Winter's Tale*: how it separates, unites and reunites certain characters; brings some characters to their death but allows others to live; creates and resolves conflict between characters; establishes, develops and resolves problems; provides opportunities for change or growth; or shapes the story by leaping over great gaps of time and place. You can explore the significance of such large patterns by focusing on a particular instance. For example, you could examine the arc of the relationship between Leontes and Polixenes. The play first introduces us to the friends in the company of Hermione. It soon physically separates Polixenes from Leontes, although Leontes continues to talk about Polixenes as his wife's co-conspirator. Sixteen years later, Leontes and Polixenes are reunited with each other (but only offstage) and finally with Hermione in the last scene. One effective approach would be to show how Leontes's reunion with Polixenes in Act Five takes its meaning from their prior unions and separations. Some questions you might ask: how do Leontes and Polixenes interact with each other in their first scene together? How would you describe Hermione's role or position in their relationship? How much of Leontes's anger and suspicion is directed at Polixenes, as opposed to Hermione? What is the effect of the sixteen-year gap that occurs before the friends' reunion? What is the significance of the way in which that reunion comes about? What kind of political or emotional significance does their reunion have? What impact does Hermione's return have on their reunion? Another approach to a plot-based argument would be to explore the significance of the deaths of Mamillius and Antigonus. Why do Mamillius and Antigonus 'have to' die? How do their deaths affect subsequent events? How would *The Winter's Tale* be a different play had they not died?

Starting with a word

Instead of tracing a large pattern as in the above examples, you might enjoy honing in on a small unit of meaning, such as a word. Begin with any word that you have come across in your reading or have recorded in your journal. Most productive for this assignment are words that are repeated throughout the play and that represent complex concepts: examples would include 'tongue', 'grace', 'honour', 'play', 'innocence/innocent', or 'traitor'. Use the *OED* to explore the seventeenth-century meanings of the word; use a concordance to identify the word's appearances throughout the play. Then formulate an argument addressing how that word illuminates some aspect of the play. For instance, let's say you have chosen the word 'traitor': 'one who is false to his allegiance to his sovereign or to the government of his country' (*OED*, traitor, *n.* 2.*spec.*). According to the online concordance OpenSourceShakesepare, 'traitor' appears six times in *The Winter's Tale*. Looking at each of those instances, you might ask the following kinds of questions. What conclusions can you draw from who is called a traitor, by whom and in what circumstances? What consequences or punishments are traitors threatened with? How do those accused of being traitors respond, if at all? What ultimately happens to each of the characters who is accused of being a traitor?

Engaging with an adaptation

Just as Shakespeare adapts Robert Greene's *Pandosto* to write *The Winter's Tale*, so recent writers have adapted *The Winter's Tale* for their own imaginative works. Advertised as a 'cover version' of *The Winter's Tale*, Jeanette Winterson's novel *The Gap of Time* (2015) takes place in contemporary London and 'New Bohemia', a southern American city in which Shep and his son Clo find an abandoned baby one rainy evening. Nike Sulway's poem 'Death, Dildoes, and Daffodils: *A Winter's Tale*' (2016) imagines the intimate relationship between Hermione and Paulina during their sixteen-year co-habitation. Especially if you enjoy creative writing, you might wish to write an essay addressing how a modern author uses *The Winter's Tale* to address major issues (e.g. female agency, family relations, abuse of power) for our own time. Whenever discussing an adaptation, you should ask yourself why the author might have chosen to write in response to an already existing text, instead of inventing an entirely new story. What choices does the writer make in borrowing or omitting from the source text? What aspects of the source text do they transform or expand upon? Also consider how much material the writer appropriates from the original text. For instance, although Winterson takes her title and certain plot features (e.g. a jealous husband, an abandoned child) from *The Winter's Tale*, her novel offers its own fully realized world, with entirely different characters and settings from Shakespeare's. Conversely, Sulway uses the characters and events of the play, imaginatively filling in the play's silence about Hermione's secret life on Paulina's estate. Following are some questions that might help you to formulate a thesis about adaptations. What is the effect of writing a new story that builds off an existing story? How does your knowledge of the original add dimension or resonance to the adaptation? Does the adaptation give you a new perspective on or understanding of the original text? Does the adaptation alter the original's genre, and with what effects? What kind of 'interpretation' does the adaptation implicitly offer in its handling of the themes, characters or plot events of the original text?

Parsing a performance

If you enjoy the performing arts, you might wish to analyse the interpretive consequences of the specific choices made in a live performance or film of *The Winter's Tale*. In other words, you would be exploring what interpretation or 'version' of *The Winter's Tale* a particular performance offers. Physical action, costuming, casting, props, setting, sound, lighting and acting can all significantly affect how we perceive particular characters or events on the stage or screen. Laurence Olivier's cinematic portrayal of Hamlet is very different from Mel Gibson's. A production of *The Winter's Tale*, to consider some examples, might make choices in casting, costuming, setting, editing or directing that serve to represent Leontes as a much more sympathetic person than you imagined from your own reading of the play. A production might use light and sound design to give the play's final scene a joyous or sombre mood. To formulate a thesis about a production, carefully observe how the company has materialized the text and focus on the significance of one or more of their major choices or directions. You might ask yourself the following kinds of questions. Has the production made any choices (e.g. in casting, setting, costuming, acting style, etc.) that seem particularly strong, impactful or surprising? Have they made major or minor changes to the text of the play? (Every live performance of *The Winter's Tale* that I have ever seen has cut the opening scene between Camillo and Archidamus). What is the effect of any changes made to the text of the play? What did you learn or discover about the play from watching this performance?

Conversing with the critics

It will come as no surprise that literary critics have widely disagreed in their interpretations of Shakespeare's plays, and *The Winter's Tale* is no exception. One way to identify an essay topic is to research which issues have inspired critical debate and to take a position in that debate. For instance, Shakespeare writes characters such as Hermione with so much nuance, complexity and openness that critics often offer different assessments of these characters' actions. According to Peter Erickson, at the beginning of the play Hermione is 'vibrant, feisty, forceful, but once accused of infidelity she adopts a stance of patience and stoic passivity' (825). Disagreeing with Erickson, David Bergeron 'find[s] no loss' of female agency later in the play, 'especially if one considers the enormous power that Hermione and Paulina wield in the last scene' (12, n.3); moreover, during the trial scene Hermione demonstrates 'great strength' (3). Does Hermione retain her power throughout the play, as Bergeron claims, or gradually lose it, as Erickson claims? Which argument do you find more persuasive, and why? What evidence could you cite to support either argument? Since this kind of essay requires researching and sifting through published scholarship on *The Winter's Tale* in order to identify a critical disagreement, only more experienced students should take it on. If you don't have much experience reading scholarship, it can be challenging to present a critic's argument accurately, quote judiciously and insert yourself into the virtual 'conversation'.

The research project

Another kind of essay can be grounded in original research of primary texts, such as the sixteenth- and seventeenth-century texts examined in relation to *The Winter's Tale* in Chapter Three. For this research project, you will explore the *English Broadside Ballad Archive*, which provides free access to over 9,000 ballads [see Further Reading]. You can search the database by keyword, such as 'marriage', 'religious concepts', 'rural life', 'politics / government' or 'children'. Using the *Archive*, find one or two sixteenth- or seventeenth-century ballads that engage with an issue you would like to explore in *The Winter's Tale*. Rich topics would include marital strife, familial discord, outspoken women, jealousy, cuckoldry, domestic violence, tyranny, courtly politics, sin, repentance, forgiveness, wonders and miracles. As we did with the historical texts in Chapter Three, you should give an account of the ballad you've chosen: describe its characters or plot, analyse its language or imagery, or explain what you find significant about its treatment of a particular topic. Then show how the ballad illuminates a similar topic in *The Winter's Tale*, paying attention to any similarities or differences of language, perspective, plot etc., that you find significant.

Choosing an essay topic II: Creative approaches

Although all good scholarship and interpretation are creative, following are some options for essay topics that stress creative writing skills.

Letter to the director

Imagine that you are an avid theatre-goer living in a community whose local theatre company produces only one Shakespeare play a year. This year the company is considering yet another production of *Romeo and Juliet*! You, however, are eager to experience a performance of *The Winter's Tale*, which you have never before seen on stage. Write a letter to the director of the company persuading them to stage *The Winter's Tale* on the grounds that the play offers a fascinating treatment of an issue still of interest to us today (e.g. women's authority, marital strife, abuse of power etc.). Define that issue carefully and quote passages from the play that clearly illustrate it. To prove your point, perform close readings of the language, imagery, metaphors etc., of the passages you quote. Your aim is to present what you find intriguing about *The Winter's Tale* in a detailed, persuasive way that will convince the director to stage the play.

The new soliloquy

Imagine you are a writer hired by a theatre company that wants to produce an 'updated' and modern English version of *The Winter's Tale*. They ask you to make any changes to the text you choose as long as they remain consistent with the original play. You decide to write a soliloquy for a character who doesn't have one, such as Paulina, Hermione, Polixenes or Perdita. Write a letter to the theatre company explaining your decision. For this assignment, you don't actually have to write the new soliloquy, although you can if you like – but in modern English, as it is very difficult to write accurately and organically in a Shakespearean idiom. Either way, your letter should explain where you would place the soliloquy in the play and what its content would be. For instance, you might explain what subject the character would be pondering, how the character's understanding of the subject might change during the course of the soliloquy, and what kind of language or imagery the character would use to explore that subject. Is the character trying to resolve a moral dilemma or decide on a course of action? Does the character reach some sort of conclusion or remain in doubt? How does your soliloquy provide new insight into why the character behaves the way he or she does in the play? You might give some examples (brief quotations) of what the character would say in the soliloquy. In any case, the soliloquy should demonstrate consistency with the character's language and behaviour elsewhere in the play. (It wouldn't make sense for Hermione to have a soliloquy in which she boasts about her sexual relationship with Polixenes). To complete this assignment, then, you will need to provide some analysis of the character as Shakespeare created him or her.

Writing the essay

An essay is typically organized into several parts: an introductory paragraph with a clear statement of thesis; several paragraphs of analysis and argument to prove the thesis; and a conclusion gesturing to the larger significance or implications of the thesis. An essay should also have a specific title that encapsulates the thesis. Below are suggestions for writing each part of the essay.

Title

It can be tricky to write an excellent title, though knowing what to avoid is half the battle. Ideally, your title will not only identify the topic of your essay (say, Leontes's tyranny) but also give your reader a sense of what you will be arguing *about* that topic. 'Leontes' tyranny' would be a weak title because it doesn't indicate what your argument about his tyranny will be. It can take some thought to formulate a title that provides a clue to the essay's thesis in a concise, punchy way that grabs your reader's interest. You should usually come up with a title *after* having completed the essay, since you will have a more accurate idea of what, precisely, your essay is about.

Ineffective titles:

- Paper on *The Winter's Tale*
- Tyranny in Shakespeare
- Leontes's Tyranny Destroys Family, Court

The first title says nothing about the content of the essay. The second title is too general and doesn't mention the text under consideration. Regarding the third example, essay titles should avoid a *noun-verb-object* structure (e.g. *tyranny-destroys-family*), which sound like newspaper headlines.

Effective titles:

- Jealousy as a Form of Tyranny in *The Winter's Tale*
- 'The Office Becomes a Woman Best': Paulina's Theory of Tyranny in *The Winter's Tale*
- Neither Good King nor Tyrant: Leontes's Imperfect Rule in *The Winter's Tale*

Consider each of these titles as offering a template for a different kind of naming strategy. What kinds of structures do these titles use, and why do they work well? How does each manage to convey the essay's thesis in a different way?

Introductory paragraph

After the title, the introductory paragraph is where you want to make a strong first impression on your reader. (As with the title, however, you should always write your introductory paragraph *after* having completed the essay, since you will only then know what kind of thesis and approach you need to introduce). Never begin an essay with a clichéd generalization such as 'Shakespeare was a great writer who lived in the sixteenth century', because such statements are irrelevant to the specific topic of your essay and will immediately bore your reader. Such sentences are essentially 'filler' that take up space without saying anything new, important or interesting. Moreover, there is no need to take such a wide perspective: your essay will not discuss Shakespeare's greatness as a writer or the many plays he wrote. Keep your focus narrow and relevant. For instance, let's say you are writing an essay titled, '"The Office Becomes a Woman Best": Paulina's Theory of Tyranny in *The Winter's Tale*'. Your introduction might begin like this: 'Why is Paulina the only character in *The Winter's Tale* who dares call Leontes a tyrant? Although it might seem strange that a royal counselor's wife, and not one of the counselors themselves, would make such an incendiary claim, Paulina is in fact a highly informed judge of Leontes' political flaws.' In just two sentences, you have grabbed the reader's attention with a pointed question, a seeming anomaly (a woman who engages in politics), and a strong claim explaining that anomaly (Paulina is qualified to engage in politics). You are also well on your way to presenting your thesis. Your reader will now want to know why you think Paulina is an informed judge of political matters: the next sentence or two can provide that information, leading to a thesis statement that elaborates the titular claim about Paulina's 'theory of tyranny'. The thesis statement will present your argument about what that theory is and why it is significant for an understanding of the play.

Thesis statement

An effective thesis statement presents a *debatable* claim: a theory, argument or interpretation about which equally well informed people might reasonably disagree. A thesis statement is never a statement of fact – something that can be simply proven to be right or wrong. What you will prove in the course of your essay is not that your claims are *right* but that they are *plausible*. Through the presentation and analysis of textual evidence, you are trying to convince your reader – it can be helpful to imagine a sceptical reader whom you have to 'win over' – that your way of interpreting what happens in the play makes sense (is believable, consistent, coherent) and offers valuable insight into the play. Building on the sample essay topic above, let's consider some ineffective and effective versions of possible thesis statements.

Ineffective thesis statements:

- Paulina accuses Leontes of being a tyrant.
- Paulina speaks to her husband differently than she does to her king.
- To understand what Paulina means when she calls Leontes a tyrant, we should consider what early modern political theorists thought about tyranny.

The first example is a statement of fact, of what literally happens in the play. A thesis would offer an interpretation of *why* Paulina accuses Leontes, at what point, with what consequences, and so on. The second example is an observation that might lead to a strong thesis if given a sharper focus. The word 'differently' is too vague because it does not specify the nature of the difference in Paulina's speech to the two men. Does she speak gently to her husband and roughly to the king? Does she speak cruelly to her husband and angrily to the king? Since the possibilities are endless, you don't want to leave your reader guessing. Moreover, even an improved version of this thesis statement – e.g. 'Paulina speaks gently to her husband and roughly to the king' – still has too much of the observational and not enough of the interpretive. Having observed Paulina's different style of address to the two men, you should next formulate a thesis about the *significance* of that difference. Why does your observation matter? How does it help us better to understand Paulina's ethics, or gender relations in *The Winter's Tale*, or the agency that an aristocratic wife might assume in courtly politics?

The third ineffective thesis statement above is a sentence that might work well in your introductory paragraph, because it explains the approach you are taking to *The Winter's Tale*: you will address how Paulina understands tyranny, and you will explore that topic by looking at discussions of tyranny in sixteenth-century texts. While it's helpful to inform your reader that you will be taking a historical approach, you still need to formulate a thesis about the *significance* of Paulina's use of the concept of tyranny, in light of those contemporary sources. Consulting contemporary political treatises can give you important insights into the early modern concept of tyranny, but you still need to explain how you will apply those insights to an interpretation of Paulina's character.

Effective thesis statements:

- Paulina calls Leontes a tyrant because she understands that only by insulting him as he has insulted her will she get him to respect her authority.
- Paulina calls Leontes a tyrant not because she wants him to reform his style of leadership, but because she wants him to accept responsibility for Hermione's death.
- Paulina's astute use of the concept of tyranny shows that she is not the stereotypical scold that Leontes makes her out to be but – even more than the king's male counsellors – a master of courtly politics.

Although these three examples make different kinds of argument, they all clearly indicate what that argument is. Moreover, they enfold into a single sentence a good deal of information about what the reader should expect from the essay. The first two examples purport to explain *why* Paulina calls Leontes a tyrant. According to the first thesis, she does so as a strategy to earn his respect. This essay might argue that, in the course of observing and interacting with Leontes, Paulina comes to understand that he responds only to aggression. If she insults him (by calling him 'tyrant') just as he has insulted her, perhaps she will earn his attention and respect, enabling her to exert more influence over him. This essay will need first to prove that Leontes typically uses insulting language with Paulina (and/or others) and that in calling him a tyrant Paulina is imitating his style of exerting authority.

The next example uses a more complex structure (*not because X but because Y*) that presents not only the essay's argument – Paulina calls Leontes a tyrant because she wants him to accept responsibility for Hermione's death – but also a different possible reading of Paulina's motives that the essay will consider and reject. One might assume that Paulina calls Leontes a tyrant because she wants him to recognize and reform his tyrannical behaviour. The writer of this essay will entertain this reasonable interpretation only to reject it in favour of the more surprising interpretation that links the accusation of tyranny specifically with Hermione's death.

The final example addresses not Paulina's reasons for calling Leontes a tyrant but rather what her ability to use that concept reveals about her political skills. Like the previous one, this thesis contains an implicit counter-argument that the essay will entertain only to refute: that Paulina criticizes Leontes because she is a 'scold', a woman who can't control her tongue. The essay will argue that far from being such a stereotypical figure of excessive femininity, Paulina is a shrewd player of courtly politics equal to or superior to the play's male courtiers. To make this argument, the writer might bring in definitions of kingship and tyranny from early modern political writers, but the thesis statement need not be clogged up by discussion of this historical approach. Instead, the thesis simply presents the argument that Paulina deploys the concept of tyranny in a politically astute way: the main paragraphs of the essay can bring in evidence from primary sources to justify this account of Paulina's facility with political terminology.

Main paragraphs

The primary purpose of the paragraphs comprising the core of the essay is to prove the thesis, using whatever methods of argumentation and analysis work best. A good paragraph tends to have three distinct parts: a topic sentence that 'signposts' (like a road sign) for the reader the direction in which the argument is going; evidence that supports this particular stage of the argument; a concluding sentence that drives home what the paragraph has proven and that possibly gestures towards the next stage of the argument (the following paragraph).

Preparing your reader for the argument to follow, a good topic sentence is crucial in establishing the main point of the paragraph. Imagine that the thesis of your essay is as follows: 'Paulina's astute use of the concept of tyranny shows that she is not the stereotypical scold that Leontes makes her out to be but – even more than the king's male counsellors – a master of courtly politics.' You might devote one main paragraph to addressing the implicit counter-argument that Paulina speaks harshly because she *is* a scold. Here is a possible topic sentence for that paragraph: 'When accusing Leontes of abusing his authority, Paulina certainly displays some traits of the stereotypical scold.' With this sentence you have announced that in this paragraph you will define some traits of the typical scold and will use evidence from Paulina's debate with Leontes to show how she manifests those traits. Having provided that analysis, you might use the concluding sentence of the paragraph to pithily sum up what you have proven: 'Aggressive and relentless, Paulina berates Leontes much like scolds were thought to berate their beleaguered husbands.' The topic sentence of the subsequent paragraph might then alert the reader to a shift in direction: 'Despite her resemblance to the stereotypical scold, however, when Paulina charges Leontes with tyranny she does so as a level-headed, temperate counsellor advising her sovereign.' Whereas the first part of this topic sentence provides a transition from the previous paragraph's discussion of scolds, the 'however' clearly signals that you are about to qualify or contradict that argument. The second part of the topic sentence explains that in the specific circumstance of charging Leontes with tyranny, Paulina acts not like a scold but like a wise counsellor. Your reader should understand that this paragraph will provide evidence of Paulina's 'level-headed, temperate' behaviour when she warns Leontes about his tyranny. Providing transitions and signposts for your reader need not mean a stilted or heavy-handed style; these rhetorical gestures can be elegantly integrated with your analysis of the text.

Doubtless the most challenging aspect of textual analysis is working with direct quotations from the play. Let's first consider some effective techniques for quoting shorter pieces of Shakespearean text. In each of the following examples, the writer has not successfully integrated quoted material into their own sentence. Each revision offers just one possible way to improve these sentences.

Original
Paulina says, 'Alas, I have showed too much / The rashness of a woman' (3.2.217-18). This quote shows that Paulina regrets her rash speech.

Revision
Paulina blames herself for displaying the 'rashness of a woman': the impulsive speech that was traditionally seen as a sign of female unruliness (3.2.218).

Original
Hermione states 'with immodest hatred / The childbed privilege denied' (3.2.100-1).

Revision
Hermione complains that Leontes' 'immodest hatred' has denied her the 'privilege' of recovering her health in bed following the birth of her child (3.2.100-1).

Original
Camillo says, 'If ever I was wilful-negligent, / It was my folly' (1.2.253-4).

Revision
Responding to Leontes' accusations of incompetence, Camillo claims that if he was ever deliberately 'negligent' in his duties, it was during a moment of unaccustomed 'folly' (1.2.253-4).

Some specific improvements made in the above revisions include removing awkward and wordy phrasing; aiming for economy by quoting only the most important words from the text; integrating quotations so as to create grammatically correct, complete sentences; providing adequate contexts for quoted material; and providing analysis in the process of quoting.

Another common challenge is performing detailed analysis of longer passages. It is crucial to understand that a passage from a play cannot in and of itself serve as evidence of any argument that you are making. Citing a passage in your essay is really a convenience for the reader: a way for the reader to access the text that you are analysing without having to turn to a copy of the play. Not the passage itself but your detailed reading of it constitutes the evidence for your argument. The basic rule here is that *a quotation never speaks for itself*. Put another way, the meaning of a quotation is never self-evident: you cannot assume that your reader knows what *you* think a quotation means or why it is important to your argument. You need to do the work of showing the reader what the quotation means and why it is important to your argument. You do that work through close reading.

Imagine, for instance, that you were writing an essay arguing that Dion and Cleomenes use religious language as a strategy to convince Leontes to remarry. As evidence for this thesis, you decide to quote and analyse the following passage in which Dion explains to Paulina the importance of Leontes's remarriage.

> DION
> You pity not the state, nor the remembrance
> Of his most sovereign name, consider little
> What dangers, by his highness' fail of issue,
> May drop upon his kingdom and devour
> Incertain lookers-on. What were more holy
> Than to rejoice the former queen is well?
> What holier, than for royalty's repair,
> For present comfort and for future good,
> To bless the bed of majesty again
> With a sweet fellow to't?
>
> (5.1.25-34)

An inadequate analysis might look something like the following:

> Dion uses a religious argument to warn about what will happen if Leontes does not remarry. He claims that instead of thinking about Hermione, who is 'well', Leontes should find a new wife.

Although this analysis is not incorrect, it is general and bland, and moreover presents the writer's interpretation of the passage as a self-evident fact needing no further explanation. That is, the writer states that Dion 'uses a religious argument' without *showing* how Dion's argument might be considered 'religious'. Remember that your reader might not see what you see in the passage. Even though to you Dion's argument might be unambiguously religious, another reader might not perceive it as religious, or might in fact disagree that it is religious. Simply stating that the argument is religious does not provide *evidence* of the thesis that the king's advisers use religious language to sway his decision.

A strong analysis of the passage might discuss some of the following details to demonstrate that Dion is making a religious argument:

- words that have a clear religious denotation or a possible religious connotation, such as 'holy', 'holier', 'rejoice' and 'bless' (look them up in the *OED*!);
- the possible allusion to the early modern concept of the divine right of kings through language such as 'sovereign', 'highness', 'royalty' and 'majesty' (here you could support your analysis by providing historical context or by quoting from a primary text, such as a speech by King James I);
- the possible allusion in 'sweet fellow' to the Protestant emphasis on marriage as a spiritual fellowship between spouses (here you could support your analysis by providing historical context or by quoting from a primary text, such as a marriage sermon);
- an analysis of Dion's claim that it would be 'holy' to rejoice that Hermione is 'well' (presumably because she is in heaven).

A strong analysis would not necessarily address every one of these points, or address them all in equal depth, but each of these points would give you the chance to work closely with the language of the passage and to show how that language provides evidence for your argument.

Concluding paragraph

There are different strategies for writing concluding paragraphs. As a reader of student work, I always appreciate concluding paragraphs that avoid a stale repetition of what the writer has already proven in the essay. It would be disappointing to read an essay arguing for Paulina's politically astute use of the concept of tyranny only to arrive at a concluding paragraph that essentially reads: 'In this essay, I have proven that Paulina is politically astute in her use of the concept of tyranny. I have proven this thesis by showing *x*, *y* and *z*....' Unless you've written a long thesis (of twenty or more pages), your reader doesn't need to be reminded of what they just read a couple of pages ago. Instead, consider the final paragraph an opportunity to continue exploring a topic that has captured your interest and, hopefully, your reader's interest. The difficultly, of course, is figuring out how to continue this exploration while simultaneously drawing your investigation to a close.

One effective strategy is to remark on the possible implications of your analysis. The hypothetical essay we've been discussing might conclude by addressing the larger lessons or 'takeaways' from having proven that Paulina is a shrewd courtier. For instance, you might observe that we replicate Leontes's own shortsightedness if we dismiss Paulina's insights simply because she has an audacious manner. Paulina's political commentary must be taken seriously, even if we find her delivery overly passionate. Alternatively, you could argue that it is precisely Paulina's understanding of the role of the emotions in political counsel that makes her advice more valuable than that of Leontes's male counsellors. Taking a different approach, you might suggest that politically shrewd women in Shakespeare such as Paulina and Lady Macbeth are often accused of manipulating powerful men, but they are in fact no more manipulative than male counsellors. It would be perfectly fine to gesture in your conclusion to a familiar character such as Lady Macbeth in order to suggest how your argument might illuminate similar circumstances in other plays or provide a broader perspective on the gender assumptions we bring to our reading of Shakespeare's strong women. Whatever strategy you adopt, the important thing is that your concluding paragraph leaves the reader with a lasting impression, just as you want your introductory paragraph to make a strong first impression.

BIBLIOGRAPHY

Primary sources

Church of England. *An Homily of Repentance and of True Reconciliation unto God. The Second Tome of Homilies.* London, 1563.
de Dominis, Marco Antonio. *The Rockes of Christian Shipwracke.* London, 1618.
Fletcher, John. *The Faithful Shepherdess.* London, 1608.
King James, I. *The True Law of Free Monarchies.* Edinburgh, 1598.
Riche, Barnabe. *The Excellency of Good Women.* London, 1613.
Shakespeare, Wiliam. *The Winter's Tale.* Ed. John Pitcher. The Arden Shakespeare. London: Bloomsbury, 2014.
Smith, Thomas. *De Republica Anglorum.* London, 1583.
Stubbes, Phillip. *The Anatomie of Abuses.* London, 1583.
Stubbes, Phillip. *The Theater of the Pope's Monarchy.* London, 1584.
Swetnam, Joseph. *The Araignment of Lewd, Idle, Froward, and Unconstant Women.* London, 1615.
Varchi, Benedetto. *The Blazon of Jealousie.* Trans. R.T. London, 1615.
Whately, William. *A Bride-Bush, or A Wedding Sermon.* London, 1617.

Secondary sources

Adelman, Janet. *Suffocating Mothers: Fantasies of Maternal Origin in Shakespeare's Plays, Hamlet to The Tempest.* New York: Routledge, 1992.
Akhimie, Patricia. 'Galleries and Soft Power: The Gallery in *The Winter's Tale*'. *Early Modern Diplomacy, Theatre and Soft Power: The Making of Peace.* Ed. Nathalie Rivère de Carles. New York: Palgrave Macmillan, 2016, 139–60.
Alpers, Paul. *What Is Pastoral?* Chicago: University of Chicago Press, 1996.

Baldo, Jonathan. 'The Greening of Will Shakespeare'. *Borrowers and Lenders: The Journal of Shakespeare and Appropriation* 3.2 (2008).
Barish, Jonas. *The Antitheatrical Prejudice*. Berkeley: University of California Press, 1981.
Barish, Jonas. 'Mixed Verse and Prose in Shakespearean Comedy'. *English Comedy*. Eds. Michael Cordner, Peter Holland and John Kerrigan. Cambridge: Cambridge University Press, 1994, 55–67.
Beckwith, Sarah. *Shakespeare and the Grammar of Forgiveness*. Cornell: Cornell University Press, 2011.
Belsey, Catherine. 'The Exiled Princess in a Sad Tale for Winter'. *In the Footsteps of William Shakespeare*. Ed. Christa Jansohn. Münster: Lit Verlag, 2005, 159–75.
Belsey, Catherine. *Shakespeare and the Loss of Eden: The Construction of Family Values in Early Modern Culture*. New Brunswick, NJ: Rutgers University Press, 1999.
Belsey, Catherine. 'Shakespeare's Sad Tale for Winter: *Hamlet* and the Tradition of Fireside Ghost Stories'. *Shakespeare Quarterly* 61 (2010): 1–27.
Benkert, Lysbeth Em. 'Faith and Redemption in *The Winter's Tale*'. *Religion and the Arts* 19 (2015): 31–50.
Bergeron, David M. 'Hermione's Trial in *The Winter's Tale*'. *Essays in Theatre* 3.1 (1984): 3–12.
Bishop, T. G. *Shakespeare and the Theatre of Wonder*. Cambridge: Cambridge University Press, 2006.
Blum, Abbe. '"Strike all that look upon with mar[b]le": Monumentalizing Women in Shakespeare's Plays'. *The Renaissance Englishwoman in Print: Counterbalancing the Canon*. Eds. Anne M. Haselkorn and Betty S. Travitsky. Amherst, MA: University of Massachusetts Press, 1990, 99–118.
Boose, Lynda. 'Scolding Brides and Bridling Scolds: Taming the Woman's Unruly Member'. *Shakespeare Quarterly* 42 (1991): 179–213.
Bradley, Beatrice and Tanya Pollard. 'Tragicomic Conceptions: *The Winter's Tale* as Response to *Amphitryo*'. *English Literary Renaissance* 47 (2017): 251–69.
Bristol, Michael. 'In Search of the Bear: Spatiotemporal Form and the Heterogeneity of Economies in *The Winter's Tale*'. *Shakespeare Quarterly* 42 (1991): 145–67.
Brown, Pamela Allen. *Better a Shrew than a Sheep: Women, Drama, and the Culture of Jest in Early Modern England*. Cornell: Cornell University Press, 1993.
Bruster, Douglas. 'The Politics of Shakespeare's Prose'. *Rematerializing Shakespeare: Authority and Representation on the Early Modern English Stage*. Eds. Bryan Reynolds and William West. New York: Palgrave Macmillan, 2005, 95–114.

Burgess, Glenn. *Absolute Monarchy and the Stuart Constitution*. New Haven, CT: Yale University Press, 1996.
Cavell, Stanley. *Disowning Knowledge in Seven Plays of Shakespeare*. Cambridge: Cambridge University Press, 2003.
Cohen, Walter. 'Prerevolutionary Drama'. *The Politics of Tragicomedy: Shakespeare and after*. Eds. Gordon McMullan and Jonathan Hope. New York: Routledge, 1992, 122–50.
Coldiron, A. E. B. '"'Tis Rigor and Not Law": Trials of Women as Trials of Patriarchy in *The Winter's Tale*'. *Renaissance Papers* (2004): 29–68.
Cooper, Helen. *The English Romance in Time: Transforming Motifs from Geoffrey of Monmouth to the Death of Shakespeare*. Oxford: Oxford University Press, 2004.
Cormack, Bradin. 'Shakespeare's Other Sovereignty: On Particularity and Violence in *The Winter's Tale* and the Sonnets'. *Shakespeare Quarterly* 64 (2011): 485–513.
Crawford, Julie. 'Women's Secretaries'. *Queer Renaissance Historiography: Backward Gaze*. Eds. Vin Nardizzi, Stephen Guy-Bray and Will Stockton. Burlington, VT: Ashgate, 2009, 111–34.
Cunningham, J. V. *Woe or Wonder: The Emotional Effect of Shakespearean Tragedy*. Denver: University of Denver Press, 1951.
Danson, Lawrence. 'The Shakespeare Remix: Romance, Tragicomedy, and Shakespeare's "distinct kind"'. *Shakespeare and Genre: From Early Modern Inheritances to Postmodern Legacies*. Ed. Anthony R. Guneratne. New York: Palgrave Macmillan, 2011, 101–18.
Das, Nandini. 'Romance and the Reinvention of Wonder in the Early Seventeenth Century'. *Seventeenth-Century Fiction: Text and Transmission*. Eds. Jacqueline Glomski and Isabelle Moreau. Oxford: Oxford University Press, 2016, 19–33.
Dawson, Anthony B. 'The Secular Theater'. *Shakespeare and Religious Change*. Eds. Kenneth J. E. Graham and Philip D. Collington. New York: Palgrave Macmillan, 2009, 238–60.
Dewar-Watson, Sarah. 'The *Alcestis* and the Statue Scene in *The Winter's Tale*'. *Shakespeare Quarterly* 60 (2009): 73–80.
Diehl, Huston. '"Does Not the Stone Rebuke Me?": The Pauline Rebuke and Paulina's Lawful Magic in *The Winter's Tale*'. *Shakespeare and the Cultures of Performance*. Eds. Paul Yachnin and Patricia Badir. Burlington, VT: Ashgate, 2008, 69–82.
Diehl, Huston. '"Strike All that Look upon with Marvel": Theatrical and Theological Wonder in *The Winter's Tale*'. *Rematerializing Shakespeare: Authority and Representation on the Early Modern Stage*. Eds. Bryan Reynolds and William West. New York: Palgrave Macmillan, 2005, 19–34.

Dolan, Frances E. 'Hermione's Ghost: Catholicism, the Feminine, and the Undead'. *The Impact of Feminism in English Renaissance Studies*. Ed. Dympna Callaghan. New York: Palgrave Macmillan, 2007, 213–37.

Drakakis, John. '"*Jew.* Shylock Is My Name": Speech Prefixes in *The Merchant of Venice*'. *Shakespeare and Modernity: Early Modern to Millennium*. Ed. Hugh Grady. New York: Routledge, 2000, 105–21.

Duckert, Lowell. 'Exit, Pursued by a Polar Bear (More to Follow)'. *Upstart* (2013). http://www.clemson.edu/upstart/Essays/1.xhtml.

Duncan, Claire. '"Nature's Bastards": Grafted Generation in Early Modern England'. *Renaissance and Reformation* 38 (2015): 121–47.

English Broadside Ballad Archive. Dir. Patricia Fumerton. Department of English, University of California at Santa Barbara. https://ebba.english.ucsb.edu/.

Enterline, Lynn. '"You Speak a Language That I Understand Not": The Rhetoric of Animation in *The Winter's Tale*'. *Shakespeare Quarterly* 48 (1997): 17–44.

Erne, Lukas. 'What We Owe to Editors'. *Shakespeare in Our Time: A Shakespeare Association of America Collection*. Eds. Dympna Callaghan and Suzanne Gossett. London: Bloomsbury, 2016, 64–8.

Felperin, Howard. *Shakespearean Romance*. Princeton: Princeton University Press, 1972.

Felperin, Howard. '"Tongue-tied our queen?": The Deconstruction of Presence in *The Winter's Tale*'. *Shakespeare and the Question of Theory*. Eds. Geoffrey H. Hartman and Patricia Parker. London: Methuen, 1985, 3–17.

Forman, Valerie. *Tragicomic Redemptions: Global Economics and the Early Modern English Stage*. Philadelphia: University of Pennsylvania Press, 2008.

Fox, Adam. *Oral and Literate Culture in England 1500–1700*. Oxford: Oxford University Press, 2000.

Friedlander, Ari. 'Roguery and Reproduction in *The Winter's Tale*'. *The Oxford Handbook of Shakespeare and Embodiment: Gender, Sexuality, Race*. Ed. Valerie Traub. Oxford: Oxford University Press, 2016, 491–505.

Gillespie, Stuart. 'Shakespeare and Greek Romance: "Like an old tale still"'. *Shakespeare and the Classics*. Eds. Charles Martindale and A. B. Taylor. Cambridge: Cambridge University Press, 2004, 225–37.

Grantley, Darryll. '*The Winter's Tale* and Early Religious Drama'. *Comparative Drama* 20 (1986): 17–37.

Gross, Kenneth. *The Dream of the Moving Statue*. Cornell: Cornell University Press, 1992.

Hamlet on the Ramparts. 'Tutorials and Guides: What Is a Folio? Act/Scene'. MIT Global Shakespeare Project: Digital Environments for

Shakespeare. Dir. Peter S. Donaldson. http://shea.mit.edu/ramparts/commentaryguides/index.htm.

Howard, Jean E. 'Shakespeare and Genre'. *A Companion to Shakespeare*. Ed. David Scott Kastan. Oxford: Blackwell, 1999, 297–310.

Hunt, Maurice. '"Bearing Hence": Shakespeare's *The Winter's Tale*'. *SEL* 44 (2004): 333–46.

Hunt, Maurice. 'Romance and Tragicomedy'. *A Companion to Renaissance Drama*. Ed. Arthur F. Kinney. Oxford: Blackwell, 2002, 384–98.

Hunt, Maurice. 'Syncretistic Religion in Shakespeare's Late Romances'. *South Central Review* 28 (2011): 57–79.

Ingram, Jill Phillips. '"You ha'done me a charitable office": Autolycus and the Economics of Festivity in *The Winter's Tale*'. *Renascene* 65 (2012): 63–73.

Jardine, Lisa. *Still Harping on Daughters: Women and Drama in the Age of Shakespeare*. 2nd ed. New York: Columbia University Press, 1989.

Jensen, Phebe. 'Singing Psalms to Horn-Pipes: Festivity, Iconoclasm, and Catholicism in *The Winter's Tale*'. *Shakespeare Quarterly* 55 (2004): 279–306.

Jones, Ann Rosalind. 'Counterattacks on "the Bayter of Women": Three Pamphleteers of the Early Seventeenth Century'. *The Renaissance Englishwoman in Print: Counterbalancing the Canon*. Eds. Anne M. Haselkorn and Betty S. Travitsky. Amherst, MA: University of Massachusetts Press, 1990, 45–62.

Jordan, Constance. *Shakespeare's Monarchies: Ruler and Subject in the Romances*. Cornell: Cornell University Press, 1997.

Jowett, John. 'Varieties of Collaboration in Shakespeare's Problem Plays and Late Plays'. *A Companion to Shakespeare's Works*. Vol. IV. *The Poems, Problem Comedies, Late Plays*. Eds. Richard Dutton and Jean E. Howard. Oxford: Blackwell, 2003, 106–28.

Kastan, David Scott. *Shakespeare and the Book*. Cambridge: Cambridge University Press, 2001.

Kendrick, Matthew. 'Imagetext in *The Winter's Tale*'. *Textual Practice* 29 (2015): 697–716.

Kurland, Stuart M. '"We Need No More of Your Advice": Political Realism in *The Winter's Tale*'. *SEL* 31 (1991): 365–86.

Lambert, Erin. 'The Reformation and the Resurrection of the Dead'. *Sixteenth Century Journal* 47 (2016): 351–70.

Langley, Eric. 'Postured like a Whore? Misreading Hermione's Statue'. *Renaissance Studies* 27 (2012): 318–40.

LaRoque, Francois. '"Nature's Bastards": The Hybridity of *The Winter's Tale*'. *Shakespeare Studies* 45 (2017): 1–12.

Leimberg, Inge. '"Golden Apollo, a Poor Humble Swain... ": A Study of Names in *The Winter's Tale*'. *Shakespeare-Jahrbuch* (1991): 135–58.

Levine, Laura. *Men in Women's Clothing: Anti-Theatricality and Effeminization, 1579–1642*. Cambridge: Cambridge University Press, 1994.

Lesser, Zachary. 'Unknowing Kind: A Response to Tanya Pollard'. *Blind Spots of Knowledge in Shakespeare and His World: A Conversation*. Ed. Subha Mukherji. Kalamazoo, MI: Medieval Institute Publications, 2019, 133–5.

Lim, Walter S. H. 'James I, the Royal Prerogative, and the Politics of Authority in Shakespeare's *The Winter's Tale*'. *The Upstart Crow* 21 (2001): 27–38.

Lim, Walter S. H. 'Knowledge and Belief in *The Winter's Tale*'. *SEL* 41 (2001): 317–34.

Loomis, Catherine. 'Bringing Justice to Bear: An Unusual 1609 Trial'. *Shaping Shakespeare for Performance: The Bear Stage*. Eds. Catherine Loomis and Sid Ray. Madison, NJ: Fairleigh Dickinson University Press, 2016, 71–86.

Lupton, Julia Reinhard. *Afterlives of the Saints: Hagiography, Typology, and Renaissance Literature*. Stanford: Stanford University Press, 1996.

Lupton, Julia Reinhard. 'Judging Forgiveness: Hannah Arendt, W.H. Auden, and *The Winter's Tale*'. *New Literary History* 45.4 (2014): 641–63.

Martin, Randall. 'Paulina, Corinthian Women, and the Revisioning of Pauline and Early Modern Patriarchal Ideology in *The Winter's Tale*'. *Shakespeare, the Bible, and the Form of the Book: Contested Scriptures*. Eds. Travis DeCook and Alen Galey. New York: Routledge, 2012, 57–76.

McCoy, Richard C. *Faith in Shakespeare*. Oxford: Oxford University Press, 2013.

McDonald, Russ. *Shakespeare and the Arts of Language*. Oxford: Oxford University Press, 2001.

McKeown, Adam. 'Rhetoric and the Tragedy of *The Winter's Tale*'. *The Upstart Crow* 20 (2000): 116–32.

McMullan, Gordon. *Shakespeare and the Idea of Late Writing: Authorship in the Proximity of Death*. Cambridge: Cambridge University Press, 2007.

McMullan, Gordon and Jonathan Hope. 'Introduction: The Politics of Tragicomedy, 1610–50'. *The Politics of Tragicomedy: Shakespeare and after*. Eds. Gordon McMullan and Jonathan Hope. New York: Routledge, 1992, 1–20.

Miller, Nichole E. 'Ambivalent Temporality and Penitential Eros in *The Winter's Tale*'. *Modern Philology* 114 (2017): 630–56.

Moncrief, Kathryn. '"Show me a child begotten of thy body that I am father to": Pregnancy, Paternity, and the Problem of Evidence in *All's Well That Ends Well*'. *Performing Maternity in Early Modern England*. Eds. Kathyrn Moncrief and Kathryn McPherson. Burlington, VT: Ashgate, 2007, 29–44.

Mowat, Barbara A. 'Facts, Theories, and Beliefs'. *Shakespeare in Our Time: A Shakespeare Association of America Collection*. Eds. Dympna Callaghan and Suzanne Gossett. London: Bloomsbury, 2016, 57–64.

Mowat, Barbara A. '"What's in a Name?" Tragicomedy, Romance, or Late Comedy'. *A Companion to Shakespeare's Works. Vol. IV. The Poems, Problem Comedies, Late Plays*. Eds. Richard Dutton and Jean E. Howard. London: Blackwell, 2003, 129–49.

Mulready, Cyrus. *Romance on the Early Modern Stage: English Expansion before and after Shakespeare*. New York: Palgrave Macmillan, 2013.

Newcomb, Lori Humphrey. *Reading Popular Romance in Early Modern England*. New York: Columbia University Press, 2002.

Newcomb, Lori Humphrey. 'Toward a Sustainable Source Study'. *Rethinking Shakespeare Source Study: Audiences, Authors, and Digital Technologies*. Eds. Dennis Austin Britton and Melissa Walter. New York: Routledge, 2020, 19–45.

O'Connell, Michael. *The Idolatrous Eye: Iconoclasm and Theater in Early Modern England*. Oxford: Oxford University Press, 2000.

O'Connor, Marion. '"Imagine Me, Gentle Spectators": Iconomachy and *The Winter's Tale*'. *A Companion to Shakespeare's Works. Vol. IV. The Poems, Problem Comedies, Late Plays*. Eds. Richard Dutton and Jean E. Howard. Oxford: Blackwell, 2003, 365–88.

Orgel, Stephen. 'The Poetics of Incomprehensibility'. *Shakespeare Quarterly* 42 (1991): 431–7.

Orgel, Stephen. 'Shakespeare and the Kinds of Drama'. *The Authentic Shakespeare, and Other Problems of the Early Modern Stage*. New York: Routledge, 2002, 143–58.

Parker, Patricia. 'Sound Government, Polymorphic Bears: *The Winter's Tale* and Other Metamorphoses of Eye and Ear'. *The Wordsworthian Enlightenment: Romantic Poetry and the Ecology of Reading*. Eds. Helen Regueiro Elam and Frances Ferguson. Baltimore: Johns Hopkins University Press, 2005, 172–90.

Pollard, Tanya, ed. *Shakespeare's Theater: A Sourcebook*. Oxford: Blackwell, 2004.

Purkiss, Diane. '"As like Hermione as is her picture": The Shadow of Incest in *The Winter's Tale*'. *Maternity and Romance Narratives in Early Modern England*. Eds. Karen Bamford and Naomi J. Miller. New York: Routledge, 2016, 75–91.

Quilligan, Maureen. 'Exit Pursued by a Bear: Staging Animal Bodies in *The Winter's Tale*'. *The Oxford Handbook of Shakespeare and Embodiment: Gender, Sexuality, Race*. Ed. Valerie Traub. Oxford: Oxford University Press, 2016, 506–22.

Ravelhofer, Barbara. '"Beasts of recreacion": Henslowe's White Bears'. *English Literary Renaissance* 32 (2002): 287–323.

Ray, Maggie Ellen. 'The Queen's Two Bodies in *The Winter's Tale*'. *The Palgrave Handbook of Shakespeare's Queens*. Eds. Kavita Mudan Finn and Valerie Schutte. New York: Palgrave Macmillan, 2018, 251–69.

Reinhart, Gordon. 'All the World's a Stage Direction: Shakespeare's First Folio for Actors'. *Scholar Talks and Keynote Presentation* 5 (2016). https://scholarworks.boisestate.edu/first_folio_talks/5.

Robertson, Lauren. '"Ne'r was dream so like a waking": The Temporality of Dreaming and the Depiction of Doubt in *The Winter's Tale*'. *Shakespeare Studies* 44 (2016): 291–315.

Rokison, Abigail. 'Shakespeare's Dramatic Verse Line'. *The Oxford Handbook of Shakespeare's Poetry*. Ed. Jonathan Post. Oxford: Oxford University Press, 2013, 285–305.

Saylor, Sara. '"Almost a Miracle": Penitence in *The Winter's Tale*'. *Enchantment and Dis-Enchantment in Shakespeare and Early Modern Drama*. Eds. Nandini Das and Nick Davis. New York: Routledge, 2017, 153–69.

Schalkwyk, David. '"A Lady's "Verily" Is as Potent as a Lord's": Women, Word, and Witchcraft in *The Winter's Tale*'. *ELR* 22 (1992): 242–72.

Schalkwyk, David. *Shakespeare, Love and Service*. Cambridge: Cambridge University Press, 2008.

Shannon, Laurie. *Sovereign Amity. Figures of Friendship in Shakespearean Contexts*. Chicago: University of Chicago Press, 2002.

Smith, Emma. *Macbeth: Language and Writing*. London: Bloomsbury, 2013.

Smith, Ian. *Race and Rhetoric in the Renaissance: Barbarian Errors*. New York: Palgrave Macmillan, 2009.

SparkNotes Editors. 'No Fear *The Winter's Tale*'. *SparkNotes.com*. SparkNotes LLC, 2005. www.sparknotes.com/nofear/shakespeare/winterstale/.

Stallybrass, Peter. 'Patriarchal Territories: The Body Enclosed'. *Rewriting the Renaissance: The Discourses of Sexual Difference in Early Modern Europe*. Eds. Margaret W. Ferguson, Maureen Quilligan and Nancy J. Vickers. Chicago: University of Chicago, 1986, 123–42.

Stevens, Andrea Ria. *Inventions of the Skin: The Painted Body in Early English Drama, 1400–1642*. Edinburgh: Edinburgh University Press, 2013.

Strain, Virginia Lee. '*The Winter's Tale* and the Oracle of the Law'. *ELH* 78 (2011): 557–84.
Strier, Richard. 'Mind, Nature, Heterodoxy, and Iconoclasm in *The Winter's Tale*'. *Religion and Literature* 47 (2015): 31–59.
Styrt, Philip Goldfarb. 'Resistance Theory, Antigonus, and the Bear in *The Winter's Tale*'. *SEL* 57 (2017): 389–406.
Sulway, Nike. 'Death, Dildoes, and Daffodils: *A Winter's Tale*'. *TEXT* 36 (2016): 1–16.
Taylor, Gary. 'Collaboration 2016'. *Shakespeare in Our Time: A Shakespeare Association of America Collection*. Eds. Dympna Callaghan and Suzanne Gossett. London: Bloomsbury, 2016, 141–9.
Thomas, Miranda Fay. '"Tremble at Patience": Constant Queens and Female Solidarity in *The Two Noble Kinsmen* and *The Winter's Tale*'. *The Palgrave Handbook of Shakespeare's Queens*. Eds. Kativa Mudan Finn and Valerie Schutte. New York: Palgrave Macmillan, 2018, 87–103.
Tiffany, Grace. 'Paganism and Reform in Shakespeare's Plays'. *Religions* 9 (2018): 1–11.
Trim, Michelle D. and Megan Lynn Isaac. 'Reinventing Invention: Discovery and Investment in Writing'. https://wac.colostate.edu/books/writingspaces/writingspaces1/.
van Elk, Martine. '"Our praises are our wages": Courtly Exchange, Social Mobility, and Female Speech in *The Winter's Tale*'. *Philological Quarterly* 79 (2000): 429–57.
Vanita, Ruth. 'Mariological Memory in *The Winter's Tale* and *Henry VIII*'. *SEL* 40 (2000): 311–37.
Villeponteaux, Mary. '"Good queen, my lord, good queen": Royal Mothers in Shakespeare's Plays'. *The Palgrave Handbook of Shakespeare's Queens*. Eds. Kativa Mudan Finn and Valerie Schutte. New York: Palgrave Macmillan, 2018, 145–60.
Waldron, Jennifer. 'Of Stones and Stony Hearts: Desdemona, Hermione, and Post-Reformation Theater'. *The Indistinct Human in Renaissance Literature*. Eds. Jean E. Feerick and Vin Nardizzi. New York: Palgrave Macmillan, 2012, 205–27.
Wells, Marion. 'Mistress Taleporter and the Triumph of Time: Slander and Old Wives' Tales in *The Winter's Tale*'. *Shakespeare Survey* 58 (2005): 247–59.
Winterson, Jeanette. *The Gap of Time: A Cover Version of William Shakespeare's The Winter's Tale*. London: Hogarth, 2015.

Further reading and resources

Guides

Several excellent guides, companions and collections cited above will reward further reading about Shakespeare's life, work, theatre and culture. I particularly recommend the following:

A Companion to Renaissance Drama. Ed. Arthur F. Kinney. Oxford: Blackwell, 2002.

A Companion to Shakespeare. Ed. David Scott Kastan. Oxford: Blackwell, 1999.

A Companion to Shakespeare's Works. 4 vols. Eds. Richard Dutton and Jean E. Howard. Oxford: Blackwell, 2003.

The Oxford Handbook of Shakespeare and Embodiment: Gender, Sexuality, Race. Ed. Valerie Traub. Oxford: Oxford University Press, 2016.

The Oxford Handbook of Shakespeare's Poetry. Ed. Jonathan Post. Oxford: Oxford University Press, 2013.

Shakespeare in Our Time: A Shakespeare Association of America Collection. Eds. Dympna Callaghan and Suzanne Gossett. London: Bloomsbury, 2016.

Shakespeare's Theater: A Sourcebook. Ed. Tanya Pollard. Oxford: Blackwell, 2004.

Websites

The Bodleian First Folio

https://firstfolio.bodleian.ox.ac.uk

This site offers a digital facsimile of a First Folio of Shakespeare's plays held at the Bodleian Library, Oxford University.

The Complete Works of William Shakespeare

http://shakespeare.mit.edu

This site offers public domain editions of all of Shakespeare's works, categorized as 'comedy', 'history', 'tragedy' or 'poetry'.

Early English Books Online [EEBO]

https://www.english-corpora.org/eebo

This open source version of the EEBO database contains over 25,000 searchable texts first published from the 1470s through the 1690s.

English Broadside Ballad Archive [EBBA]

https://ebba.english.ucsb.edu

Directed by Patricia Fumerton at the University of California at Santa Barbara, this public database contains over 9,000 searchable ballads from the sixteenth and seventeenth centuries, including text, art and music.

Internet Shakespeare Editions

https://internetshakespeare.uvic.ca

This site provides various open-access Shakespeare resources, including old-spelling and modernized editions of plays, materials from over 1,000 film and stage productions, and scholarly accounts of theatre, society, politics, art, literature and music in early modern England.

JSTOR Understanding Shakespeare

https://www.jstor.org/understand/shakespeare

This site provides complete texts of Shakespeare's plays, with individual passages linked to scholarly articles and book chapters that cite that passage. Complete articles can then be downloaded if your school or library subscribes to the JSTOR [short for 'journal storage'] digital library. For *The Winter's Tale*, over 800 articles are linked.

The Folger Shakespeare

https://shakespeare.folger.edu

This site provides free online versions of the Folger Shakespeare editions of Shakespeare's plays and poems.

Folger Shakespeare Library

https://www.folger.edu/online-resources

Several databases are available to the public. Among them, Shakespeare Documented offers the largest collection of primary source materials relating to Shakespeare's life. The Digital Image

Collection (or LUNA) provides access to over 100,000 images from the Library's collections, including books, theatre memorabilia, manuscripts and art.

MIT Global Shakespeares Video and Performance Archive

https://globalshakespeares.mit.edu

Directed and edited by Peter Donaldson at the Massachusetts Institute of Technology, this database provides access to several hundred performances of Shakespeare from all over the world.

OpenSourceShakespeare Concordance

http://www.opensourceshakespeare.org/concordance

This searchable concordance of Shakespeare's complete works allows you to search for any word either in full or in part form (e.g. 'play' will capture 'plays', 'playing' and 'played'). Search results are broken down by play or poem and present the word in the context of the passage in which it appears, along with line citation.

Oxford English Dictionary

https://www.oed.com/

With a subscription at a school or public library, you can look up any word in the English language and see how its meanings have changed with time, along with representative quotations (often from Shakespeare!).

Shakespeare in Quarto

https://www.bl.uk/treasures/shakespeare/homepage.html

This British Library site provides free access to 107 copies of the 21 plays by Shakespeare that were printed in quarto form prior to 1642. Plays are presented in facsimile and can be viewed one at a time or through side-by-side comparison.

Shakespeare's Globe

https://www.shakespearesglobe.com/learn/research-and-collections/archive-collections

This site provides free access to the performing arts archive of the Globe Theater in London, including the Performance Archive (documenting performances at the Globe), the Moving Image and Audio Archive and the Library Collections (featuring scholarly publications and rare books).

Shakespeare's Words

https://www.shakespeareswords.com

Especially useful if you don't have access to the *OED*, Ben Crystal's and David Crystal's site provides a glossary of all the words in Shakespeare's texts that have since changed their meaning (or no longer exist) in Modern English. An audio option lets you hear how these words are pronounced. There are other research tools as well, such as a thesaurus and a database of word families (e.g. 'accord'/ 'accordant'/'accordingly').

World Shakespeare Bibliography

www.worldshakesbib.org

With over 132,000 records, The World Shakespeare Bibliography is searchable database of Shakespeare-related publications and performances worldwide since 1960.

Editions of the play

Along with the individual Arden Shakespeare volumes cited in this book, excellent individual editions of *The Winter's Tale* have been published by the Folger Shakespeare Library (ed. Barbara Mowat and Paul Werstine; see also 'The Folger Shakespeare' in *Websites* above); Bedford Texts and Contexts (ed. Mario DiGangi); Oxford University Press (ed. Stephen Orgel); Cambridge University Press (ed. Susan Synder and Deborah T. Curren-Aquino); and Pelican (ed. Frances E. Dolan).

www.ingramcontent.com/pod-product-compliance
Lightning Source LLC
Chambersburg PA
CBHW061837300426
44115CB00013B/2415